Serve It Cold!

A Cookbook of Delicious
Cold Dishes

Serve It Cold!

A Cookbook of Delicious Cold Dishes

By June Crosby

and

Ruth Conrad Bateman

GARDEN CITY, NEW YORK

DOUBLEDAY & COMPANY, INC.

ACKNOWLEDGMENTS AND CREDITS

The authors wish to thank friends, associates and restaurants around the world for their help and inspiration with recipes and ideas that have enriched this book immeasurably. We are grateful to our mutual friend Corris Guy, Director of Consumer Service, Helms Bakeries, for bringing us together in this enterprise, and to Elena Quinn for her patience and expertise in typing our manuscript. We deeply appreciate the encouragement and understanding at all times that we have been given by our editors at Doubleday, Miss Louise Gault and Miss Clara Claasen. And finally we salute the following, who have provided the beautiful full-color photographs in our book:

Knox Gelatine, Inc.—Front jacket—Princess Crab Mousse, Minted Melon Ring and Cherries in Port.
Calavo—Plate No. 1—Pineapple Pupus, Papaya and Prosciutto and Crudités with Tapenade.
Woman's Day magazine, photograph by Robert E. Coates—Plate No. 2—Jambon Persillé with Mustard Fruit Mayonnaise, Chicken Breasts en Gelée and Dilly Tuna in Jellied Egg Ring.
Hellman's/Best Foods Mayonnaise—Plate No. 3—Greek Salata.
Sunkist Growers, Inc.—Plate No. 4—Orange Trifle.
Several of the recipes in this book first appeared in *House & Garden* magazine, Copyright © 1968 by The Condé Nast Publications, Inc. We are grateful to them for their use.

To our families,
who have lived with and loved our
cold cooking.

Contents

Items indicated by an asterisk * may be located by consulting the Index.

Items indicated by a dagger † will be found in Glossary and Shopper's Guide.

Introduction

It isn't everyday that you can turn the corner and find a new idea. Still, we all hope to do just that. Fads in cookbooks have almost covered the bookshelves, with books for every national cuisine and one for every food. However, there is a whole new world of cooking that is relatively unexplored—the elegant, cool, serene world of cold cooking.

Here for the first time in one neat volume are marvelous cold dishes from all over the world. Cold meats, fish and fowl, glittery aspics, mousses and airy soufflés, iced soups and salads of course, and a selection of special sandwiches and cold drinks. The appetizers are imaginative but not complicated, and we've tried to take the mystery out of the pâtés and terrines included. Our collection of chilled and frozen desserts, though not vast, was chosen with great care and each is a special recipe you'll want to use often.

Aside from their good looks and special flavor, cold dishes have a unique appeal. *They can all be made ahead*, sometimes even days in advance, and served at your leisure and convenience. Tucked away in the refrigerator hours before a party, cold dishes give the hostess a secure, relaxed feeling. Who cares if the cocktail hour lengthens? The chicken aspic or the salmon mousse will be just as delicious and attractive as at the planned serving time. And usually, foods made especially to be chilled are prepared when you are less hurried and can thus be more imaginative and creative.

Needless to say, cold dishes aren't necessarily to be served in hot weather only. One cold course is always a refreshing spot in any meal—an icy soup to start it off, a frozen dessert to end it or a beautiful fish aspic in the middle. And since the cold dish can be prepared ahead, it's the easiest of all on the cook.

The inspiration for our recipes has come from everywhere . . . the Scandinavian smörgåsbord and the luxurious Russian zakusky, colorful Italian antipasto and timeless French hors d'oeuvres. Exotic ideas for eggplant, cucumbers, melons, ices and such came from the Middle East and Mediterranean countries. And unusual ways with fish, spices, tropical fruits and vegetables we've learned from the Islands and Pacific peoples.

To offset the exotic and unusual, we've included famous cold dishes from the Classic Cuisine. Many were specialties of the lavish cold buffets presented by Escoffier when he reigned over the kitchens of the great London Savoy. All have been adapted and simplified to fit our modern kitchens and equipment, our present-day markets and cooking know-how.

Some of the most exciting recipes in our book are those from our personal collections picked up from restaurants, hotels and friends around the world. They range from a unique cocktail appetizer called Trout Antipasto to a delicate caramel custard made with Grand Marnier discovered in a tiny, offbeat bistro in France.

The proper presentation of a cold dish cannot be stressed too much. A great deal of thought has been given to the decorations, garnishes and accompaniments we suggest, and we suggest them for practically every recipe. They should be important, and dramatic when possible, with a fresh shiny look. They should be neat and symmetrical, and not look haphazard or labored-over. And above all, garnishes should be delicious to eat and a definite part of the dish itself.

Though this is not a menu book, we often give suggestions and ideas for suitable accompaniments following many of the recipes. And we have included a few sample menus to show how our cold dishes fit in with other foods. In working with cold dishes, we find a menu of cold foods needs to be carefully balanced and dramatically presented with considerable thought given to variety in texture, color and flavor—even more so than in a mixed menu. On occasion you may wish to serve a complete cold meal with only hot coffee or tea as a contrast. At other times, a cup of clear hot soup or a basket of hot bread or rolls may be the element needed to balance your cold dishes. Again, your beautiful cold creation could be the one cold food you need in an otherwise hot meal.

This is a book we feel, not only for the connoisseur, but for every busy homemaker who appreciates excellence in food and likes to serve it. While a number of the party and classic dishes require time, we've balanced them with more than an equal measure of interesting dishes that can be put together quickly and easily with the many shortcuts we've devised.

Modern refrigerators and freezers, blenders and mixers make quick

work of many time-consuming processes formerly involved in making aspics, ices, glazes, sauces and such. Cold foods can be held
at peak perfection for hours, or days as the case may be. Saran film
enables us to keep delicate poached fish and poultry moist, salads
crisp and bright, a sauce or aspic fresh and shiny. That miracle
worker, the electric blender, we've used endlessly in the production
of soups, sauces, mousses, ice creams and frosty drinks. And though
we tell you how to make some of the basic stocks, how could we
have written this book without the convenience of canned bouillons,
consommés, meat stock bases and the like?

We wondered at first how we'd ever collect enough cold dish
recipes to fill a book, now after more than a year and a half of
testing and searching through culinary writings from all over the
world, we know we've hardly scratched the surface. But we have
attempted to bring you the best and most exciting of the world's
cold dishes, both old and new, in do-able, contemporary language.

To help you, the first section of this book is devoted to basic
information we feel is essential in making cold dishes well. Special
equipment, stock and aspic making, new modes in gelatine cookery,
molds and garnishes—all are discussed. A careful reading of this will
give you a background of what cold cooking is all about. Then you
can go full-speed ahead with confidence when you get into the
recipes.

To all cool cooks, our serendipity.

JUNE CROSBY
RUTH CONRAD BATEMAN

CHAPTER 1

Know-how for Cold Dishes ~~~

GOOD EQUIPMENT MAKES GOOD COOKS

While good tools may not make you the best cook in the world, they help considerably, and make cooking easier and more fun. We don't know a single great or even just "passing-good" cook or chef who doesn't have good utensils which he uses and cares for meticulously. The use of proper tools can make the difference between a homemade, amateurish look in your finished dish and the slick polished effect obtained by the pros.

To make the delicious cold dishes in this book, you need the same good assortment of heavy pots and pans, sharp knives, measuring tools you use in regular cooking. But, in testing and working out our recipes, we found certain equipment was very important and used over and over again. A basic list of these is given and also a few luxury items such as terrines and fancy molds to add as you can afford them.

Refrigerators—A frost-free model with an automatic ice-maker would be perfect, but any good refrigerator will be adequate. It should be large enough to cope with regular day-to-day fresh foods and still, with a little juggling, have room to chill a large mold, a buffet platter of sliced meat and vegetables being glazed with aspic or a dessert that needs to chill overnight. Two refrigerators, one to use for special cold dishes and beverages, a big turkey, etc., would be the greatest luxury we can imagine.

Freezers—A separate freezer or the combination refrigerator-freezer having two separate doors, each with its own temperature controls, is the ideal choice. In either of these you can quick-freeze foods and keep ready-frozen foods over long periods of time, while the freezer compartment of your conventional refrigerator is suggested only for storing frozen foods for short periods.

Blender—A good one with a large container and at least two speeds is a great time saver and practically indispensable for sauces, mousses and many of the soups and desserts.

Electric Mixer—Elementary! Not only functions in its own role for speedy mixing and blending, but with a meat grinder and juice attachment can take over those chores and many others. A manually operated beater serves well also.

Knives—Good knives are important and most basic are a paring knife, a heavy French chef's knife (once you learn to use it you'll never be without it for mincing, chopping, etc.) and a long thin slicing knife for picture-pretty thin slices of ham, tongue, turkey, beef. Extras that are nice for our recipes include a medium-size, slender knife for boning meats and poultry, a serrated bread knife for fancy sandwiches and a smaller serrated tomato and fruit knife for thin, symmetrical slices.

Food Mill—Purées vegetables, fruits, raw fish, etc., where the electric blender process is not wanted.

Meat Grinder—With several blades, a must for pâté mixtures, some mousses, sandwich fillings.

Meat Thermometer—The only way to be positive of internal meat and fish temperatures.

Graters—An assortment is nice in both fine and medium. Also helpful is the grater or slicer that makes neat, even slices of cucumber, carrots, etc. for decorations and garnishes.

Egg Slicer—Essential for even, symmetrical slices for aspics and decorations.

Parsley Mincer—A French-made Mouli device that seems to mince parsley as nothing else does.

Chopping Boards—One small and portable, one large. Where else would you make those pretty garnishes?

Juicer—Manual or electric, a must for beverages, desserts, molds.

Vegetable Peeler—Useful in making garnishes and decorations also.

Strainers—Coarse and fine needed for clear aspics, etc.

Wire Whisks—A small one for smoothing sauces and custards, large balloon whip for the fastest, lightest egg whites obtainable.

Kitchen Shears—Use endlessly for quick snips of herbs, paper liners, etc.

Garlic Press—Saves time and fingers. Gives stronger flavor than minced or chopped so use accordingly.

Melon Ball Cutter—Especially nice for desserts, fruit compotes, some vegetable garnishes.

Large Kettle—At least 10- to 12-quart size for stocks, court bouillons.

Decorating Bag—With star, round and ribbon tubes for mayonnaise and whipped cream flourishes.

Cooky Cutters and/or *Truffle Cutters*—In miniature sizes for fancy aspic shapes and other decorations.

Molds—One ring mold is pretty basic and they come in sizes from 3 cups to 3 quarts. At least one fancy type mold and a set of individual small molds make a nice assortment for fancy jellied salads, aspics and desserts.

Wooden spoons, kitchen forks, ladle, broad and narrow spatulas, rubber scrapers, accurate measuring spoons and cups, mixing bowls, plus an assortment of heavy pans with tight lids go without saying.

Extra Luxuries

Fancy Molds—A fish-shaped mold for some of the fish aspics and mousses, a melon mold for fancy salads, desserts and also bombes, and a straight-sided charlotte mold or a spring-form pan for chilled or frozen ladyfinger desserts. Many of these are available in inexpensive, lightweight, copper-washed aluminum.

Soufflé Dishes—Straight-sided, porcelain dishes for cold soufflés and mousses. Small ramekins in same shape for eggs in aspic, and similar small delicacies served in the dish.

Terrines—Oval or rectangular molds of porcelain, pottery, glass or enameled cast iron for pâtés, terrines and galantines.

Fish Poacher—The long, narrow (and expensive) French *poissonnière* or a similar deepish pan large enough to hold a whole fish.

Ice Cream Freezer—Electric or hand-turned is a nice extra if you enjoy making old-fashioned homemade ice cream.

Poultry Shears—Extra heavy. A great help in disjointing fowl, splitting bones, etc.

Ice Crusher—A bed of crushed ice is a cool and effective way to display iced shellfish, fruits and melons, vegetable relishes, chilled soups and frozen desserts. Some blenders have attachments that crush ice.

GELATINE COOKERY, UPDATED

Natural gelatine is a substance found in bones, particularly veal and beef knuckles, shanks and such. Flavorful jellied stocks or aspics result when these are boiled with seasonings, meats and herbs. By the turn of the century, this natural animal protein had been refined into unflavored granular gelatine, which is now commercially packaged in convenient pre-measured packets of approximately 1 tablespoon each.

Unflavored gelatine is simple and easy to use and is considered *de rigueur* in classic molds and aspics. It is sugar-free and you flavor it and vary it indefinitely with your own choice of liquids, fruits, vegetables or meats and seasonings. (Packaged gelatin dessert products are presweetened and flavored.) We hope that the information on methods and basic proportions outlined here will aid you in following our recipes and encourage you to make up some of your own.

Basic Gelatine

One envelope unflavored gelatine will gel 2 cups of liquid, which may be water, stock, milk, wine, juice, cream, etc. Stock, however, is considered necessary for a true aspic and details on this subject are covered in the following section on Aspics and Stocks. Other liquids may be used for gelatine salads, desserts and the like.

For Cold Liquids. Sprinkle gelatine over cold liquid in saucepan, then stir constantly over low heat until liquid is clear and gelatine completely melted.

For Hot Liquids. Sprinkle gelatine over ½ cup cold liquid; let stand a few minutes to soften. Add boiling hot liquid (1½ cups) and stir until completely dissolved. Add desired seasonings; cool or chill and use as directed in specific recipes.

Adding Solid Ingredients. Basic gelatine or aspic must be chilled until it is beginning to set and thick enough to support the solid materials before they are added. We usually say, until gelatine is syrupy thick, as apt a term as we can find. Up to 1½ cups of chopped, minced or small pieces of well-drained fruits, vegetables, meats, fish, etc., may be added to basic 2-cup recipe.

Tall or Large Molds. Use no more than 1½ to 1¾ cups liquid for each envelope unflavored gelatine. Consider cream (before it's whipped), sour cream, thin fruit purées, etc., as part of the liquid.

Sweetened Gelatine

Fruit gelatines, desserts and some salads call for sugar, usually ¼ to ⅓ cup for each 2-cup recipe of basic gelatine. Mix dry gelatine and sugar, then pour boiling hot liquid over it, the same as you do with packaged flavored gelatins. Stir until it is dissolved. *Or,* combine dry gelatine and sugar mixture with the cold liquid and stir over low heat until clear. Sugar liquifies and this should be considered in computing your proportion of liquids to gelatine, especially if an excessive amount of sugar is used as in a large or tall mold.

Quick-set-Gel

Speed up the chilling time by using frozen juices, fruits or soup, ice cubes or ice cream for part of the liquid in basic gelatine. Details are given in specific recipes in Salads and Desserts.

Blender-Gel

Another speedy method that cuts out many of the time-consuming details of chopping, mincing, etc., and simplifies combining gelatine with liquids. Specific recipes are given in Salads, Desserts and some of the main dish mousses. Basically gelatine is softened in cold liquid directly in blender container, then boiling liquid blended in. Or, gelatine and boiling liquids are blended immediately in blender on low speed. Vegetables, fruits, nuts, etc., are added in pieces and blended until they are chopped, minced or completely puréed.

ASPICS AND STOCKS

A shiny, crystal clear aspic is beautiful to look at and a delicious cool eating experience. Actually, aspic is a well-seasoned jellied meat or fish stock with enough gel or body to stand up perky and firm on the plate yet taste tender and melting in the mouth. In the classic sense, all cold dishes which use jellied stock of one sort or another as the basis of the dish itself are called aspics.

When the jellied stock is used as a sparkling film to cover a molded dish, a chilled fish or a colorful arrangement of sliced meat and vegetables, the dish is more often referred to as *en gelée* or in jelly. The aspic or jelly, the terms are synonymous, is also used as a glittery decoration for cold foods when it's chopped, cubed or cut in fancy shapes.

To make a good aspic, start with a good stock made from scratch or canned bouillon, consommé, chicken broth or bottled clam juice. We use the canned stocks in many of our recipes because it's faster, though more expensive. When accented with herbs and special seasonings, and occasionally with wines, they are delicious. But you should know how to make a basic homemade aspic stock. In addition to being cheaper it can be more personally seasoned for the specific dish. Also, you can freeze it to have on hand when you need it. In making certain recipes, especially fancy decorated molds, it will be necessary to use Clarified Stock.*

MEAT STOCK

You can save up meat bones and freeze them till you have enough for a good stock. Or some markets sell bags of soup bones containing veal knuckles, and beef or veal shin and marrow bones.

4 pounds beef and veal bones, cracked or chopped (mixture should include some veal knuckles for gelatine content, some meat for flavor, but no lamb or pork bones)
2 onions, peeled and quartered
2 carrots, scraped and cut in chunks
Handful celery and tops, sliced

Small handful parsley
1 bay leaf
4 whole cloves
6 whole black peppercorns, lightly crushed
1 tablespoon salt, or to taste
½ teaspoon each dried thyme, tarragon and marjoram leaves
1 clove garlic, optional
2 tablespoons tomato paste

Put bones and meat in large 8 to 10 quart kettle. Cover with cold water and heat to simmering. Skim the foamy scum that rises to the top for about 5 minutes. Add remaining ingredients with the herbs and spices tied loosely in cheesecloth. Skim as necessary when liquid simmers again. Cover loosely and simmer, with just a bubble or two breaking the surface, for 4 or 5 hours. Replenish with boiling water occasionally, if necessary. Strain stock into bowl. Cool, uncovered. Then cover and refrigerate overnight. Lift off fat layer. (If time does not permit chilling overnight, skim off fat with spoon or a bulb baster. Then drag strips of paper toweling across top to blot up every drop of fat.) Makes 2 quarts.

Note: This makes a rich, full-bodied stock, which may or may not gel naturally, depending on the bones used. To be on the safe side, unflavored gelatine is added when using stock in all aspic recipes.

QUICK BEEF STOCK

To 3 cans (about 10½ ounces each) beef bouillon, add ½ cup each chopped carrot and onion, ½ cup port or Madeira wine and an herb bouquet of 4 parsley springs, a handful celery leaves, ¼ bay leaf and ¼ teaspoon each dried thyme and marjoram leaves tied loosely in cheesecloth. Simmer gently 20 to 30 minutes. Strain. Makes about 1½ pints.

CHICKEN STOCK

Follow directions for Meat Stock* substituting 4 to 5 pounds chicken backs and wings or stewing fowl for the beef and veal bones. Omit thyme, garlic and tomato paste. Add 2 thick lemon slices and 2 teaspoons dried tarragon leaves. Strain, cool and degrease as directed. Makes about 2 quarts.

QUICK CHICKEN STOCK

Follow directions for Quick Beef Stock* substituting 3 cans (or equivalent measure) chicken broth. Substitute dry white wine or sherry for port or Madeira, omit thyme and add 1 teaspoon dried tarragon leaves. Makes about 1½ pints.

BASIC COURT BOUILLON

You can poach fish beautifully in plain salted water. However, some herbs and lemon, wine or vinegar are usually added depending on the flavor of the fish itself. Cold fish dishes call for an extra measure of seasoning.

2 quarts water	4 sprigs parsley
¼ cup white wine vinegar	1 bay leaf
2 teaspoons salt	6 whole black peppercorns,
(approximately)	lightly crushed
1 onion, sliced	½ teaspoon dried thyme
1 carrot, sliced	leaves

Combine ingredients and simmer 20 to 30 minutes before using. Makes about 2 quarts.

WHITE WINE COURT BOUILLON

The addition of white wine and compatible herbs is especially desirable if cooking liquid is to be used later as an aspic or glaze for cold fish.

Omit vinegar from Basic Court Bouillon.* Add 1 quart dry white wine, 6 whole cloves, 1 teaspoon dried tarragon leaves, 1 extra sliced onion and carrot, a long strip of lemon peel and 1 more teaspoon salt. Simmer 30 minutes. Makes about 2½ quarts.

QUICK FISH STOCK

Substitute 4 cups bottled clam juice for 1 quart of water in White Wine Court Bouillon.* Reduce salt to 1½ teaspoons. Makes 2½ quarts.

FISH STOCK OR FUMET

If you wish to make a rich, deeply flavored fish stock for aspics and special cold dishes in the true classic style, ask your fish dealer for a pound or two of lean, fresh (or frozen) fish heads, bones and trimmings. Any light fish, not too strongly flavored, will do—halibut, flounder, sole or similar is fine. Combine with ingredients for White Wine Court Bouillon* and heat to simmering. Skim, then simmer 30 to 40 minutes. Strain and refrigerate. Makes about 2½ quarts.

CLARIFIED STOCK

Clear, brilliantly transparent stock is essential for a beautiful aspic. All stocks—meat, fish or chicken—may be clarified this way.

2 quarts cold, fat-free stock
3 egg whites
3 egg shells, crushed

Put stock in large saucepan. Beat egg whites lightly and stir into stock along with shells. Heat slowly to boiling, stirring constantly with wire whisk or slotted spoon. This takes 15 to 20 minutes and is a rather boring, but necessary chore. When mixture comes to a full boil, the sediment will be on top in a thick scummy layer with the clear liquid below. Set pan aside, undisturbed for 15 minutes. Then pour stock through strainer lined with several layers cheesecloth wrung out of cold water. Let drain undisturbed about 15 minutes. Cool, uncovered, and chill or use immediately. Makes 6 cups.

Note: If wine, tomato juice, tomato paste, meat extracts, etc., are to be used with the stock in an aspic, add these before clarifying stock. Keep proportion of liquid to egg white the same.

CRYSTAL ASPIC

Multiply or divide amounts according to needs of recipe.

1 quart Clarified Stock* (Meat, Fish or Chicken Stock*)
2 envelopes unflavored gelatine

If you find your stock makes quite a stiff jelly after being chilled overnight, reduce gelatine above to 1½ envelopes, except in making aspic for a glaze or garnish. Sprinkle gelatine over cold stock in saucepan (or, if stock is hot, sprinkle gelatine over ¼ cup cold water to soften, then add to stock). Stir over low heat until clear and gelatine is melted. Cool and use as directed in specific recipes. Makes 1 quart.

FISH ASPIC GLAZE

White Wine Court Bouillon*   *3 egg whites*
* or Fish Fumet**   *3 egg shells, crushed*
3 envelopes unflavored gelatine

If you plan to glaze fish in an aspic or jelly after poaching it in White Wine Court Bouillon* or Fish Fumet,* boil the liquid rapidly to reduce it to about 2 quarts very rich stock. Chill and skim off any fat. Clarify by following directions for Clarified Stock,* using egg whites and shells. Measure. For 6 cups, sprinkle gelatine over ½ cup cold water and add to clarified stock. Stir over low heat until clear and gelatine is melted. Tint at this point if you wish. Cool and chill until ready to use. Use as glaze and garnish for cold fish. Makes about 1½ quarts.

TO LINE A MOLD WITH ASPIC

Nothing is quite so impressive, particularly for a cold buffet table, as aspics of various kinds, salads, mousses and even desserts chilled in a mold lined with clear jelly. When unmolded, the transparent jelly sheaths the whole mold in a shimmering film, cool and beautiful.

Aspics made of clarified stock or other clear liquids are always used so the food itself shows through the colorful design of truffles, pimientos, green herb leaves or whatever you choose glitters and sparkles handsomely.

The amount of jelly needed varies with the size and shape of the mold, but 2 cups of Crystal Aspic* or a basic gelatine recipe is ample for the average 4- to 6-cup mold. Aspics made with stock set up very quickly, so chill thoroughly, then work with small amounts, keeping rest cold, but out of refrigerator. Chill the mold icy cold. In a small bowl set in a bowl of ice cubes or cracked ice, chill about 1 cup of the aspic until syrupy thick. Remove from ice and set mold in the bowl of ice. Pour in a little of the syrupy aspic; tilt and rotate mold slowly to coat the inside all over with a film of jelly which sets almost at once. If decorations are used (suggestions for materials and designs are given later) dip in syrupy aspic and arrange carefully on set layer. Chill a few minutes, turning mold in ice, until decorations are set.

As needed, chill more of the aspic until syrupy; then spoon carefully into mold, tilting and rotating mold slowly until decorations are covered completely and set. Spoon in more aspic (keeping it thick but spoonable by setting in bowl of ice or pan of warm water as necessary) until lining is about ¼ inch thick. Chill mold until lining is sticky firm, almost at once. It is now ready to fill with mousse, gelatine or aspic mixtures.

DESIGNS IN BOTTOM OF MOLDS

A quick way to give sparkle and sheen to many of your molded dishes is to set a colorful design in a layer of clear jelly on the bottom *only* of the mold. Fruit gelatines and salads, molded creams and other fancy desserts as well as meaty aspics and fish molds all look prettier for this glamor treatment.

Pour a thin layer of cool Crystal Aspic* or basic gelatine* into bottom of mold. Chill layer until sticky firm as above and the balance of aspic or gelatine until it is syrupy thick. Arrange design with materials suggested under Decorations for Molds* on top of sticky firm layer. Cover carefully with a thin layer of syrupy thick aspic. Chill again until sticky firm. Fill mold carefully with aspic mixture, salad, fruit, mousse, etc.

DECORATIONS FOR MOLDS

You can be fanciful or simple, flowery or formal in designs for jellied molds. Let your own taste, the character of the dish itself and the material you have dictate the choice. The great Carême, chef of kings in the nineteenth century, set the pace with his extremely ornamental molds and established forever the fact of cooking and garnishing as an art. Designs in aspic take time, but they need not be intricate, and fortunately, they can and must be done ahead when you can set your own pace.

Many of the classic dishes use rather formal designs of truffle cutouts, tarragon leaves and such. But simple flowers, curlicues, neat rows, pinwheels, outlines, circles or an all-over confetti effect can be achieved with the materials below after a little practice. A set of tiny French truffle cutters for fancy shapes and a sharp knife for squares, diamonds, julienne strips, etc., are handy to have. All the slices, strips, etc., should be small, neat and thin. The same designs and materials may be used to decorate foods that are glazed with aspic such as a whole fish or chicken breasts.

Truffles—Expensive, but unique. Fancy shapes or slices used in elegant formal designs.

Black olives—Round slices, shapes or slivers used same as truffles.

Pimientos—Fancy shapes, strips, dots, squares, diamonds, triangles for formal designs, flowers, confetti effect.

Pickles—Strips, slices or fancy shapes from crisp sweet varieties or gherkins.

Radishes—Thin overlapping slices for neat rows and geometric designs, fancy cutouts for flowers, etc.

Cucumbers—Thin overlapping slices, peeled or not, for rows, geometric designs, circles. For a scalloped edge, score unpeeled cucumber deeply with fork from end to end, then slice into rounds.

Carrots—Cooked or raw in round slices, thin strips, curlicues, fancy shapes for flowers or geometric designs.

Green pepper—Strips or fancy shapes for leaves, stems, geometric designs.

Hard-cooked eggs—In round slices, crescents, strips, fancy shapes or petals from whites, dots from yolks or forced through a sieve "mimosa-style" for flower designs, borders.

Pimiento-stuffed green olives—Round slices or quarter rounds in formal and flower designs.

Chives, scallions, green onions or tender green of leeks—In slender strips as leaves or in formal designs.

Lemon, orange and lime peel—In fancy shapes for leaves, stems, petals and strips or dots for formal designs.

Parsley, watercress, mint, tarragon or other suitable and attractive herb leaves—In flower and formal designs. Wash leaves and dip in hot water. Blanch in cold water and blot dry on paper towels.

Mushrooms—Raw or cooked in thin lengthwise slices. Dip raw slices in lemon juice. Use in overlapping rows, outlines.

Fruits—Small pieces such as grapes, cherries, pineapple tidbits, kumquats, etc., may be used in a mold completely lined with aspic, but more often these are used in a mold with aspic or jelly and decorations on the bottom *only*.

Pâté de foie gras—Chilled and sliced or cut in small designs, or thin ovals of tongue, ham, white meat of chicken, shrimp, crab legs and such may be used in bottom or around sides of aspic-lined molds together with some of the above decorations.

ASPIC AS A GARNISH

Glittery shapes—Pour Crystal Aspic* in a layer ½ inch thick in shallow pan. Chill until set. Turn out on board and cut into stars, crescents, diamonds, rounds, etc., with cooky or truffle cutters. Use on platter around cold meats, fish, molds.

Chopped aspic—With heavy knife chop aspic coarsely and tumble like jewels on platter around chilled foods—a mousse or glazed fish, perhaps.

Sieved aspic—For another shimmering cool effect, force aspic through coarse strainer or sieve and place in heaps on platter around cold meats, fish and the like.

Use aspic garnishes alone or alternate with other colorful items—tiny whole carrots or balls, green beans in clumps, asparagus spears, artichoke hearts or filled artichoke bottoms, filled cucumber, lemon or orange boats, tiny whole tomatoes or wedges or slices, or bouquets of watercress, parsley or dill studded with radish roses, tiny flowers, egg slices, cucumber or lemon slices, carrot, turnip or celery petals.

TO UNMOLD AN ASPIC

Metal molds chill more quickly and are easier to unmold than porcelain or other materials. Some cooks like to oil molds very lightly before filling to facilitate unmolding and several of our recipes suggest this. It's especially helpful for creamy molds and such. But, to avoid dulling the sparkle of a clear jelly layer, it's best to simply dip molds in cold water before filling them.

After aspic or gelatine mixture is chilled firm, usually 4 hours or more, chill a serving platter of suitable size and rub over it with wet fingertips so the aspic can be slid into proper position when unmolded. Loosen aspic in several spots around edge with small narrow spatula, tilting and rapping the mold to let in air. Then dip mold quickly (and we mean very quickly) in and out of very warm water two or maybe three times to depth of contents. Wipe outside of mold with towel. Invert wet plate on top of mold; then holding plate and mold together with both hands, flip your wrists over so mold is on top. Still holding with both hands, shake downward to release aspic, then lift off mold. If mold clings, cover with a hot, wet towel until it frees itself, or quickly repeat the dipping operation. If outside of aspic softens during this caper, return the unmolded aspic to refrigerator to firm up until you're ready to garnish and serve. Obviously, all gelatine mixtures should be unmolded on a plate and returned to refrigerator until serving time whether they need a firming up or not.

GARNISHES

The right garnishing separates the "pros" from the novices, and here we hope to give you a crash course in this art. Serving foods cold demands particular attention to their presentation . . . many recipes already have their own built-in garnishes; in others, we recommend compatible accents. Oftentimes part of the name of the dish, like our Asparagus *Mimosa** (egg) and Jambon *Persillé** (Ham in Parsley Aspic) will tell you about the trimmings. Some garnishes, and there are elaborate embellishments and myriad methods, are not altogether necessary for household use . . . even though impressive.

If you have an arty hand and sculpturing fruits and vegetables is your dish of tea, that's great, but it's not the whole idea. Bear in mind the thinking of that fine French chef Carême; his logic concerning garnishing is as good today as it was in the early 1800s. He warned, "Cold dishes are everything in themselves, or they are nothing. The man of talent brings out all their inherent beauty; the man without taste detracts from it and makes them insipid."

Here then is our capsulized course in garnishing cold foods. A garnish must always blend with the flavor of the dish. It must add to the appearance and in the case of cold foods, the simpler the treatment, very often the better.

Often the use of a fruit or vegetable does double duty as a garnish and holder. Nature's own convenient and attractive packaging shows up in such recipes as Artichoke Stuffed with Crab Meat Dip,* Roquefort Mushrooms* and Lemon Ice in Lemon Shells.*

Cold food decoration is recommended in our recipes to save you endless flipping of pages to check what goes with what. In addition, we feel that some basic training regarding their treatment is important . . . so . . .

Parsley . . . like a basic black, is always in good taste. It should be washed, dried *thoroughly*, then chopped; or held together bouquet fashion, while stem ends are trimmed.

Watercress . . . is more fragile than parsley, so don't purchase it too far ahead of time. Trim stems off, remove yellow leaves and use as a bouquet or spray.

Dill and mint . . . not fragile like watercress, but they should be washed, dried and then chopped or used in bunches as other greenery. Dill as a single spray gives a very feathery effect. Mint in short sprigs gives a much coarser look.

Lemons and limes . . . when they're not in wedges, they are thinly sliced. One effective way is to slit each slice to the center, then twist one side toward you and the other away; this gives a light 3-dimensional look. If wedges are used, a dipping of the one cut side in chopped parsley or dill is most attractive.

Cherry tomatoes . . . may be used whole, cut in half, marinated in French dressing or even scooped out and filled with a pâté, mayonnaise or the ultimate . . . caviar.

Radishes . . . cut like roses, of course. Trim off stem, leave about 1 inch. Slice root end off and with sharp knife cut outside layer in petal-shaped strips from tip to stem end (to about ¼ inch from bottom) so that 5 or more sections stand out like flower petals. Chill radishes in ice water until they "bloom."

Celery . . . curled. Cut stalks into short 2 to 3 inch pieces. Slice lengthwise, about two-thirds of the way down stalk, making several cuts. Chill in ice water until curly.

Peppers . . . in rings, strips or cups. Crosswise rings may be sliced from top of pepper. After seeds and partitions are removed, these thin rings are colorful decorations. A wider slice may be used as a ring to hold groups of vegetables such as carrots (cut lengthwise), asparagus or green beans. With a slice off the top and the inside cleaned out, peppers are excellent food containers.

Pickles . . . small cucumber pickles may be "fanned." Cut 4 to 6 very thin slices from tip almost to stem end. Leave each slice still attached at stem end. Press on the end lightly to "fan" it.

Pimientos . . . these flashy bits of color are diced or cut in strips. Dry thoroughly between paper towels before using, since they come packed in oil.

Truffles . . . you need a small cutter set for these. Truffles are expensive, but worth their black accent and distinctive aroma. They should be sliced very thinly.

Olives . . . the pitted and stuffed varieties are often used for garnishing purposes. They may be sliced or cut in fancy shapes like truffles. Whole olives, black or green, make a beautiful accent on any platter.

Eggs . . . hard-cooked eggs have an endless number of uses, if a white or yellow color effect is desired, and a bland flavor. The French "mimosa" makes an attractive and useful garnish. It usually means sieved egg yolk lightly drifted over cooked vegetables, a salad or mold. Chopped egg whites and parsley may be included, if you wish.

Other effects are chopped or coarsely grated whites (sometimes like the large scales of a fish), or whites cut into fancy shapes with small cutters. Also, the egg may be quartered, sliced, cut into eighths or the yolk removed and the white stuffed with a variety of fillings.

And don't forget . . . the simple effect of a platter garnished with separate clumps of vegetables on lettuce leaves, grouped around a central feature. Or balls scooped from melons. Or the fruits and vegetables that lend themselves to imaginative boats or cups. Thinly sliced meat given a twist into a cone-shape, fastened with picks; a dab of cream cheese—or for a fancy effect, thinned cream cheese, softened butter or mayonnaise may be forced through a pastry tube into the cones in swirls or rosettes. And the value of chopped aspic, or for that matter, of sauces galore!

Most important to the end result, however, is that the garnish be complementary to the dish. As such it should be planned with the other ingredients to be a total delight to taste and sight. The field is endless, yet the basis is simplicity.

SEASONING AND SERVING COLD DISHES

The appearance and presentation of cold dishes is stressed throughout this book. More important still is flavor. Unless the dish tastes delicious, the shiny coat of aspic and the handsome garnish are useless. Many of our recipes call for an extra amount of seasonings and spices with directions to taste and season on the *plus* side. Though chilling mellows and ripens flavor in a number of foods, when they're made into mousses, aspics, creamy molds, rich pâtés and the like, the flavors are often blunted or blanded. Cream, which is used in many dishes of this sort to give pleasing delicacy and lightness, also has a blunting effect on the essence of the meat or fish itself.

In making our cold dishes, then, please do taste all along as you work and adjust seasonings when you've finished. And in nearly every case, season on the plus side, but with care and discrimination. We don't mean for you to dump a tablespoon of nutmeg in a delicate sauce for chicken, but a discreet pinch of the right spice or herb—or wise amounts of monosodium glutamate in some cases— often will change it from blah to exquisite.

This is a book of cold dishes and everything in it is chilled or frozen. But *cold* or *chilled* does not mean *icy!* The flavors, and texture as well, will be improved if cold meats, fish and such are removed from the refrigerator 10 to 15 minutes before they are served. And you will find the bouquet enhanced and the texture more pleasing if frozen desserts, especially ices and mousses, are taken out of the freezer several minutes before they are served.

CHAPTER II

Appetizers

Appetizers are fad-ish, and now, like a song of the times, something new is happening to pre-dinner delicacies. Our shrinking world has brought about an exchange of foods and customs, and there's a surge of creativity on the upswing too. Here's a sampling of marvelous appetizers from near and far, and we hope it will help you plan your menu-setting snacks . . . for appetizers are the real pacesetters of a menu. They can be "nibble food" or a separate meal, depending on what's coming next.

The cocktail party, as such, is strictly an American custom. To most Europeans, pre-dinner appetizers are just that . . . a course to be eaten at the table before soup or the main dish. The French hors d'oeuvres *variés* run in the hundreds and are often so substantial they make excellent main dishes for luncheon or supper. To name a few, a good pâté, marinated meats and fish—eggs in aspic and deviled, shellfish by the plateful and crisp, raw vegetables served with a pungent dipping sauce. Garnishing is an art and often edible flowers like nasturtiums, violets and chrysanthemums are used.

The antipasti of Italy are similar in variety, but with dozens of spicy sausages and wonderful prosciutto added. Melons and figs are beautiful there, and fish and shellfish are in abundance. Pickled vegetables, some spicy others hot, often form the edible garnish on a platter of Italian appetizers.

All Scandinavian countries have their own name for what we know as smörgåsbord, a buffet table primarily intended for sandwich-making. The idea has expanded, including more and more items, and sometimes people enjoy a smörgåsbord as a unique, complete buffet dinner . . . desserts are often included. Popular among their appetizers are herring, anchovies, dilled shrimp, Gravlax (a marinated salmon), liver pâtés, cheeses, vinegared vegetables, Anchovied Eggs

. . . and with it all Scandinavians sip a cordial glass of iced akvavit (caraway-flavored apéritif), followed by a beer chaser!

The Russian zakusky, a similar table, is served in a room adjoining the dining room. It is substantial and intended to be a meal-before-a-meal. Herring, elegant fresh caviar, Pickled Mushrooms,* Eggplant Caviar* (a vegetable spread), Salad Olivier,* smoked salmon, pâtés and pickled vegetables, white and black bread and one hot dish is the usual for a small gathering. To toast it all, Russians serve shot glasses of straight chilled vodka . . . no wonder they need appetizers of festive proportions!

Greek mézethakia are intended to be eaten out-of-hand and on foot . . . perhaps these are the forerunners of the nibble foods so typical of the American cocktail party! They usually include stuffed grape leaves, fabulous goat cheeses, a caviar spread or dip, pickled vegetables, smoked fish, toasted walnuts and olives, of course. Greeks like their ouzo (aniseed-flavored apéritif) or Greek wine with their appetizers.

Chinese dim sum are often a complete disguise . . . usually a flower-like arrangement of removable bite-size pieces of vegetables, cold meats and fish. Traditionally in China they begin a dinner with four cold dishs at the dining table. Colors and shapes are all important; Jellied Lamb would provide a "brown" tone, fish the white and raw or pickled vegetables, the bright spots.

The zensai of Japan are artfully appealing and served at the dining table too. While nibbling the crunchy pickled foods, Sashimi* (raw fish) or sushi (cold, lightly vinegared rice combined with vegetables or fish), the Japanese sip thimbleful amounts of sake, a fermented rice beverage.

What's going on at these dinners beyond and across the Atlantic or Pacific is worth exploring . . . this chapter can be your introduction to new menus, foods and customs. As every good hostess knows, strange and tasty dishes make good-food conversation, and ultimately, a successful party. Long after the festivities are over, guests will be talking about the first time they ever ate raw fish . . . and liked it!

Above all else, remember "cold" is the easy way to serve appetizers and be sociable while doing so.

PICKLED MUSHROOMS

Of all the ways the Russians serve mushrooms, this most always appears on their zakusky tables. These also fit beautifully in an Italian antipasto or French hors d'oeuvres service.

*1 pound small (button)
fresh mushrooms
¼ teaspoon salt
1 cup tarragon white wine
vinegar
¼ cup water
3 cloves*

*1 bay leaf
1 teaspoon cracked
peppercorns
2 teaspoons salt
1 clove garlic, thinly sliced
(optional)
1 tablespoon salad oil*

Wash mushrooms quickly; trim stems close to caps. Reserve stems. Drop mushroom caps into a saucepan containing 2 cups boiling water and ¼ teaspoon salt. Simmer 5 minutes. Scoop out caps; strain and remove excess liquid. Add stems to this broth; let simmer until it amounts to about 1 cup. Discard stems; save liquid for future use in soups, sauces, etc. In another saucepan combine remaining ingredients, except oil. Heat to a boil. Pack drained mushrooms in clean pint glass jar. Pour strained pickling mixture over caps. Float oil on top. Seal at once. Under refrigeration these mushrooms will keep a month or more. Give them a week to adopt pickling flavor before serving. Shake jar to distribute oil. Makes 1 pint.

ROQUEFORT MUSHROOMS

A spirited Roquefort filling in delicate raw mushrooms.

*2 dozen bite-size fresh
mushrooms
Salt and lemon juice
¼ cup dairy sour cream
2 ounces Roquefort or blue
cheese
2 teaspoons Worcestershire
sauce*

*2 teaspoons grated onion
½ teaspoon curry powder
¼ cup chopped pecans or
macadamia nuts
Tiny tips watercress*

Rinse mushrooms quickly then drop into lightly salted water with a few drops lemon juice. Drain, pull out stems and blot mushrooms dry on paper towels. Blend rest of ingredients except watercress; fill mushroom caps. Put on serving plate and cover with saran film; chill. At serving time, decorate each mushroom with a tip of watercress. Makes 12 servings of 2 mushrooms each.

ARTICHOKES SAN REMO

Make these ahead and serve as cocktail ballast, as part of the antipasto plate or as salad on top of crisp greens.

½ cup dry white wine
1 teaspoon salt
2 slices unpeeled lemon
4 whole cloves
3 whole peppercorns, crushed
1 bay leaf

1 teaspoon fennel seeds[1]
1 teaspoon coriander seeds
2 packages (12 ounces each) frozen artichoke hearts
Olive oil, lemon juice, finely cut parsley

In saucepan combine wine, 1 cup water, salt, lemon, plus herbs and spices tied loosely in cheesecloth. Bring to boil and simmer gently 10 minutes. Add artichoke hearts; simmer 5 to 10 minutes, until just crisp-tender. Cool in liquid overnight. Drain and layer in dish with a light sprinkling of olive oil, lemon juice and parsley. Cover and refrigerate several hours. Serve at room temperature. Makes 3 cups.

[1] Fennel and anise are popular flavors in many Mediterranean countries. If you do not like their licorice-like tang, substitute ½ teaspoon rosemary or oregano leaves, or 1 teaspoon gentle sweet marjoram.

PINEAPPLE PUPUS

From Hawaii—simple and unresistible. Guests always wonder what makes *this* pineapple so flavorful, yet unsugared. It is an old Chinese custom, and a good one to know about.

1 *ripe fresh pineapple*
1 *quart water*
2 *teaspoons salt*

Slice pineapple in half, through the green top to the bottom. Cut center core from each half and discard it. Carefully remove pineapple meat from each half, severing in two lengthwise pieces. Leave outer shell intact to resemble boats. Cut pineapple meat into ½ ×1-inch-size chunks. Refrigerate in covered container. About 15 minutes before serving, place chunks in chilled salt water bath; drain. Replace pieces in pineapple boats. Serve with picks.

CRUDITES WITH TAPENADE

The French way with crisp raw vegetables and a spirited dip named for *tapena,* the Provençal for capers.

Include some of the more unusual vegetables such as fennel and Belgian endive if you like, but don't forget pearly sticks of celery and turnip, bright young radishes with curly leaves for handles, crisp julienne of golden carrot, cherry tomatoes and crescents of delicate avocado. Prepare everything except avocado; chill in plastic bags. Just before serving, halve, peel and seed avocado. Cut crosswise into crescents; halve crescents. Sprinkle with fresh lime juice. Cradle vegetables in deep tray banked with finely chipped ice. Serve with bowl of Tapenade.*

Tapenade

Whizz in blender 1 whole egg, 1 teaspoon Dijon mustard and part of 3 teaspoons lemon juice. Add by droplets or in fine stream ½ cup olive or salad oil whizzing until an emulsion is formed, as in mayonnaise, or sauce thickens slightly. Gradually whizz in 1 clove garlic, chopped; 1 bottle (6 tablespoons, drained) capers; 1 tin (2 ounces) anchovy fillets, chopped. Lastly whizz in slowly ½ cup oil and the remaining lemon juice blending until sauce is creamy and thickened. Add more lemon juice if needed. Sauce will be lighter and a little thinner than mayonnaise. Makes 1½ cups.

Note: Quick Tapenade may be made by blending the capers, anchovies, garlic, mustard and lemon juice into 1 cup good mayonnaise.

ARTICHOKE STUFFED WITH CRAB MEAT DIP

A decorative flower-like artichoke serves as a receptacle for a well-seasoned crab dip, the petals are the dippers. Very San Francisco.

3 large artichokes (about 4 inches at base)
1 tablespoon lemon juice
1 teaspoon salt
½ cup crab meat (fresh, canned or frozen)
2 tablespoons lime juice
½ package (3 ounces) cream cheese
3 tablespoons mayonnaise
1½ teaspoons grated onion
1 small clove garlic, crushed
½ teaspoon finely chopped chives
Dash Tabasco
½ teaspoon Worcestershire sauce

To *prepare artichokes:* Wash and discard outer leaves. With a knife remove stems and with kitchen shears snip about ½ inch from thorny tips of each leaf. Cook in about 2 inches of boiling water, to which lemon juice and salt have been added. Cook covered for 25–30 minutes, until base can be easily pierced by fork. Remove and drain thoroughly, upside down. Refrigerate. When chilled, prepare one artichoke to be used as container for dip. Remove choke carefully, do not let outer leaves fall. Push out center leaves, so as to pull out inner, pale, thorny ones. Scrape away fuzzy choke with spoon or grapefruit knife. Remaining outside leaves should be substantial. Use other artichokes' leaves as dippers.

To prepare dip: Marinate crab meat in lime juice for 1 hour. Beat cream cheese and mayonnaise until smooth. Add onion, garlic, chives and sauces mixing well. Fold in crab meat. Cover with saran film. Refrigerate.

To serve: Place prepared artichoke in center of large round platter; fill with dip. Distribute leaves of other artichokes around petal fashion. Provide a bowl nearby for discarded leaves. Makes 4 to 6 servings, or more if other hors d'oeuvres are served.

Dining Table Appetizer: Use 6 small artichokes (with chokes removed from each). Double the crab meat filling. Makes 6 servings.

PIQUANT AVOCADO DIP

Anchovy and avocado—provocative with potables.

2 *soft-ripe medium avocados*
1 *cup dairy sour cream*
2 *teaspoons grated onion*
2 *teaspoons lemon juice*
1 *tin (¾ ounce) flat anchovy*
  fillets, minced

½ *teaspoon seasoned salt†*
Salt to taste
Crisp fried, quartered tortillas
  or large corn chips

Halve avocados, remove seed and skin. Dice avocado into bowl and mash with fork. Blend in sour cream, onion, lemon juice, anchovies and enough of their oil to make dip of a pleasing taste and consistency. Add seasoned salt and salt to taste. Serve with crisp tortilla quarters or corn chips. Makes about 2½ cups dip.

Make-ahead Trick—With most all avocado dips or spreads such as this, cover with saran film placed directly on surface of dip to exclude air. Chill. If needed at serving time, stir in a few drops green food coloring to give mixture the soft pale green color of avocado.

SOUSED CAMEMBERT

Years ago we first experienced marinated Camembert through our good friend, the late Helen Evans Brown, one of the most imaginative cooks and writers we've ever known. We've since seen many variations. It's a knockout appetizer or dessert, and is also excellent made with American-born Liederkranz or a similar soft cheese.

1 (8 ounce) soft, ripe
  Camembert
½ to 1 cup dry white wine,
  such as Chablis or Riesling
1 stick (¼ pound) sweet
  butter

½ cup toasted blanched
  almonds or filberts,
  finely chopped

Put cheese in small bowl and barely cover with wine. Cover and marinate overnight. Drain off excess wine, and carefully scrape off the grayish-brown crust. Blend cheese with soft, sweet butter until smooth, cover and chill until firm enough to shape. On cheese tile or serving board, reshape in original form or a roll. Coat completely with nuts. Refrigerate until a few minutes before serving. Cheese should have an opportunity to develop its bouquet, but butter in mixture should remain firm-ish. Serve with crisp crackers. Makes about 1 cup spread.

CAVIAR

The most elegant and precious of all hors d'oeuvres is caviar. And the most highly prized and expensive of that is the fresh Beluga caviar. This gray to black caviar, the roe or eggs of the large sturgeon fish, usually costs from $3.50 to $4.00 an ounce. It's available in fancy foods shops in practically every large city.

Preserved lumpfish, paddlefish or whitefish roe or caviar is available everywhere at a fraction of the price of the sturgeon caviar. The name of the fish is always on the label if it's other than sturgeon, but you'll know by the price. All are delicious and seem elegant.

Least expensive of all is red caviar, the large colorful eggs or roe of salmon. You can use it anywhere and everywhere for bright touches of color and flavor. In fact, all the less expensive caviars can be used to give a luxury look and taste to hors d'oeuvre platters, cold soups, garnishes, salads, egg dishes, open-face sandwiches, garnishes for molds and the like.

To Serve Caviar, it must be kept thoroughly cold in a container embedded in cracked ice. Both the fresh and the preserved may be served directly from the tin or jar embedded in ice. However, many like to rinse the preserved caviar lightly first to remove salt and oil, drain briefly on paper towels, then place in a glass bowl to be put in ice. Thin, crisp hot toast and butter, and chilled vodka or dry champagne are the traditional accompaniments. Some of us also like the small bowls of extras to add at will—fresh lemon wedges for a drop or two of juice, chopped onion and hard-cooked egg.

SWORDFISH ESCABECHE

Pickled Swordfish

A delicious low-calorie appetizer which practically makes itself. The firm, meatlike texture of swordfish is especially suitable for this pickling treatment.

2 cups white distilled vinegar	½ teaspoon dill seeds, lightly crushed
2 cups water	
1 lemon, thinly sliced	1¼ teaspoons salt
3 bay leaves	2 onions, sliced
1 dozen whole black peppercorns	1 pound swordfish steaks (about ¾ inch thick)
1½ dozen whole allspice	

In medium saucepan combine all ingredients except one onion and the fish. Simmer 30 minutes. Add fish; bring to boil and simmer gently until fish is white and opaque (3 to 5 minutes for fresh swordfish, 4 to 6 for frozen). Lift carefully from liquid with slotted spoon; cool and cut into cubes. Place in glass or earthenware dish mixing gently with remaining sliced onion. Add hot vinegar mixture. Cover and refrigerate, at least overnight. Serve on cocktail picks. No sauce is necessary, but for those who want one provide a bowl of mayonnaise or sour cream lightly seasoned with Maggi seasoning† and a touch of garlic. Makes about 1½ pints.

SASHIMI

Uncooked Fish

If you like oysters or clams on the half-shell, you'll like this Japanese appetizer. The fish must be very, very fresh and the dipping sauce pungent . . . then it's a gourmet's delight.

1 pound fresh raw fish, boned
(tuna, sea bass, red snapper
or other firm-fleshed, white-
meat fish)
1½ teaspoons grated fresh
ginger root†

¾ cup soy sauce
¾ cup thinly shredded
daikon†
Shredded lettuce or
watercress tips
Crushed ice

Remove all skin and dark meat from fish. Cut across fish on a slant, making strips about 1½ inches long by ¾ inch wide and no thicker than ⅛ inch. Chill. Combine ginger and soy sauce. Grate or shred daikon (Japanese name for large white radish). Wrap in saran film and chill. Prepare lettuce or watercress and distribute greens on oval-shaped platter. Leave one end clear for radish and sauce. Just before serving intermingle greens with ice. Lay thinly sliced fish in one or more overlapping rows on greens. Heap grated radish at platter's end, add a small saucer to hold the ginger-soy sauce. Serve with picks. Pieces of fish should be swished into sauce, then dipped into radish to eat. Makes 12 servings.

GRAVLAX

Swedish Marinated Salmon

This colorful dish is one of Sweden's most popular smörgåsbord specialties and is very easy to make. It looks and is served much like smoked salmon, but actually is raw fresh salmon marinated or "cured," if you wish, in salt, flowery-flavored fresh dill and coarse pepper. You have to taste this delicacy to know how different and delicious it is. Fresh salmon and fresh dill are required so make it only when these are available in your markets.

3 pounds fresh, center-cut salmon
1 bunch fresh dill (at least 2 cups coarsely cut)
1½ tablespoons whole black peppercorns

¼ cup sugar
¼ cup coarse salt (kosher or sea salt†) or regular salt
Swedish Mustard Sauce*

Have fish dealer split piece of salmon in two, remove bones but leave skin on. Wash dill, shake dry and blot on paper towels. Cut coarsely enough dill to cover one of the salmon pieces in a thick layer. Crush peppercorns coarsely between two sheets waxed paper with heavy rolling pin. Combine with sugar and salt. Rub some of salt mixture into fish on all sides. Lay few pieces dill in glass or pottery dish; on top place one piece of salmon, skin-side down. Cover with cut dill and rest of salt mixture. Top with second piece of fish, skin-side up, and lay a few pieces dill over it. It looks like a fat dill sandwich. Cover with saran film or foil, then a plate or lid. Weight lid down with several cans of food to compress fish. Refrigerate 3 days, turning fish every 12 hours and basting inside and out with the marinade that accumulates in the dish. Keep fish covered and weighted.

To serve, drain fish and scrape off seasonings. Blot dry with paper towels and place, skin-side down on attractive carving board. Slice very, very thinly on a slant, as is done with smoked salmon, cutting down to the skin. With knife detach slices from skin and serve with Swedish Mustard Sauce.* Good with Cucumber Salad* and dark rye bread and butter as appetizer or part of smörgåsbord. Makes a dozen, or even more, servings with other dishes.

Swedish Mustard Sauce

Traditional with Gravlax, but a superb partner for other cold fish or meat dishes.

2 tablespoons brown prepared mustard†	¼ cup vinegar
	¾ cup salad oil
1 teaspoon dry mustard	¾ teaspoon salt
¼ cup sugar	White pepper

With wire whisk blend mustards, sugar and vinegar. Gradually whisk in oil until sauce is creamy smooth and thickened. Season with salt and a little white pepper. Cover and chill before using. Beat again before serving. Makes 1 cup.

SHRIMP ARNAUD

Chef Louis La Mothe, master chef at Arnaud's Restaurant in New Orleans, created this sharply seasoned marinated shrimp dish. It has been adopted and frequently altered by hostesses all over the United States. Taste, and do likewise.

Marinade:

1 teaspoon salt	2 teaspoons prepared creole horseradish†
½ teaspoon sugar	
1 teaspoon paprika	¼ cup minced celery
1 clove garlic, crushed	¼ cup minced shallots, chives or green onions
⅓ cup tarragon or basil flavored vinegar	
⅔ cup olive oil	¼ cup minced parsley
2 tablespoons prepared creole mustard†	

2 pounds cooled, boiled shrimp

Mix marinade in pint jar: First put salt, sugar, paprika in, then garlic and vinegar. Shake well. Add oil and shake again. Add mustard and horseradish, shake vigorously. Add fresh greens, shake again, then pour over shrimp. Marinate in refrigerator overnight, or as much as a couple of days. Stir and turn occasionally. Serve with cocktail picks. Makes 6 to 8 servings.

TROUT ANTIPASTO

Crosby men are handy with a rod and reel and gourmet with a knife and fork. This is one of their recipes, and is best if made with trout or salmon freshly caught by a member of the family . . . there is much conversational mileage between the fish story and this flavorful appetizer!

1 medium onion, chopped
4 tablespoons olive oil
2 cups canned tomatoes
2 or 3 carrots, thinly sliced
1 green pepper, chopped
8 pimiento-stuffed green olives, sliced
1 stalk celery, chopped
1 tablespoon finely chopped parsley

2 tablespoons capers
1 teaspoon sugar
1 teaspoon salt
½ teaspoon pepper
1 clove garlic, crushed
6 whole cloves
2 bay leaves
1 (4 pound) trout or 3 to 4 pounds salmon fillets (use frozen, if necessary)

Sauté onion in 2 tablespoons oil until limp, not browned. Add remaining ingredients except for cloves, bay leaves and trout. Tie cloves and bay leaves in cheesecloth; add to vegetables. Simmer about 15 minutes. Meanwhile prepare trout. It is best if, when freshly caught, the big vein down back of fish is removed; if this has not been done, do so first. Then proceed to skin trout. Place fish in large pan and pour boiling water slowly over fish, especially along cut edges. Lift off head and fins, skin will peel off easily. Carefully remove bone and cut fish into small pieces. Season and sauté trout pieces lightly in remaining 2 tablespoons oil until golden brown. Add to vegetables and simmer only until carrots are done. Do not overcook. Discard bag of herbs. Spoon saucelike mixture into refrigerator containers and cool. Chill overnight. Serve as an appetizer accompanied by assorted pickled vegetables, olives and sausages . . . Italian style. Makes about 4 cups.

EGGS EASY

Uses for hard-cooked eggs can stretch as far as your imagination. As is, they are a neat, self-packaged food, good on a picnic with just a sprinkling of salt and an ice-cold bottle of beer. But in addition, there are spreads, salads and infinite variations on the stuffed egg theme. To top it off, sieved yolks make a sunshiny garnishing called "mimosa," that brightens any food.

The thing is, do hard-*cook* your eggs; don't even call them hard-*boiled!* That expression automatically implies "tough" . . . something an egg should never be. If you're without an automatic egg-cooker, follow these suggestions for good-looking and -tasting eggs. Take the eggs out of the refrigerator early; let them reach room temperature before cooking. Heat enough water in a suacepan to cover the eggs; as soon as it boils rapidly, lower each egg into the water on a large spoon. Reduce heat to a simmer. Time the cooking from when simmer stage starts; cook them 10 to 12 minutes. *And,* don't ignore them. While they simmer on, turn them over at least four times . . . this centers the yolk. When time is up, plunge the eggs into a cold water bath, this keeps that 5 o'clock greenish shadow from forming around the yolks. Also, the steam that forms between egg and shell in this temperature change makes peeling them all the easier.

Eggs Mollet is the soft-cooked method referred to in some of our recipes. The same simmering process as above is followed, up to a point . . . the time. . . . Eggs Mollet are cooked only 3 to 6 minutes. The yolks are supposed to be soft and the whites firm. They should be plunged into cold water with a stream of cold water running over them until they are thoroughly chilled. Then carefully, gently crack the shells and peel the eggs.

POACHED EGGS

Pour enough water into saucepan or skillet to cover eggs and add a tablespoon vinegar for each quart. Heat to boiling. Break very fresh egg into small dish. With spoon held upright in boiling water, stir it around to make a whirlpool; drop egg into it. White will almost immediately cover the yolk and the movement of the water

and the vinegar will help to keep the shape neat and oval. Simmer
4 minutes. White will be firm and the yolk soft. Remove with slotted
spoon to pan of cold water. Trim off any taggy bits of white. Keep
in cold water or drain and refrigerate until ready to use. If you are
poaching quite a number of eggs, you may dispense with the whirlpool bit and drop second egg into water as soon as white has
filmed over the yolk of first egg. Remove each as soon as it is cooked.

STUFFED AND SAUCED EGGS

A pretty way to start a formal dinner. Mustardy-flavored eggs go
well with speckled-green herb sauce . . . nice change too.

6 *hard-cooked eggs*   *Dill Cream Mayonnaise**
½ *teaspoon salt*   *or Sauce Verte**
1 *teaspoon Dijon mustard†*
3 *tablespoons finely chopped*
  watercress

Peel and halve eggs crosswise. Remove egg yolks; mash them and
sprinkle with salt. Add mustard and watercress. Stuff the whites.
Press halves together snugly. Slice off a piece of wide bottom of
eggs to make them stand up, dome-shaped. Place on serving dishes;
cover and chill. Prepare Dill Cream Mayonnaise* or Sauce Verte*;
pour sauce over eggs just before serving. Makes 3 to 6 servings
(one egg is usually ample for an appetizer).

STUFFED EGGS, PATE DE FOIE GRAS

These eggs go beautifully with champagne on a formal buffet.

6 *hard-cooked eggs*   2 *to 3 tablespoons heavy*
½ *teaspoon salt*   *cream*
3 *tablespoons pâté de foie*   *Pimiento*
  gras

Peel and have eggs lengthwise. Remove yolks; mash them and sprinkle with salt. Mix yolks and pâté with enough cream to make it

workable. Overstuff the whites with the mixture, use a spoon to pack it in or force it through a pastry tube. Garnish with specks of pimiento. Makes 6 to 12 servings.

ANCHOVIED EGGS

These Swedish eggs aren't "devil-ish," but they are de-lish!

6 hard-cooked eggs
¼ cup mayonnaise
2 tablespoons anchovy paste
1 tablespoon lemon juice
1 teaspoon sugar
¼ teaspoon salt

Fresh dill, if available
1 can (2 ounces) boneless anchovy fillets
Shredded red cabbage or lettuce cups

Cut eggs in half, crosswise or lengthwise; carefully remove yolks. Mash yolks, add next five ingredients and blend together. Trim a thin slice off bottom of egg whites, so they will stay put and not rock on a platter. Fill whites with anchovy mixture. Force it through a pastry tube, if you have one, making a swirling effect. Garnish each with a tiny sprig of dill and one curled or flat anchovy fillet. Place on a bed of shredded red cabbage or lettuce cups. Makes 12 servings.

EGGS EN GELEE

Eggs in aspic are timeless in appeal and can be varied ad infinitum. They make a handsome first course, and are equally effective for luncheon when slices of ham, tongue, foie gras and the like are added. If you don't have fresh tarragon, try our method with the dried herb to coax out that elusive tarragon flavor.

2 cups clear chicken broth
1 teaspoon dried tarragon leaves
1 shallot or green onion, chopped
1 envelope unflavored gelatine

Few watercress leaves (or parsley or tarragon)
4 chilled Poached Eggs* or Eggs Mollet*
Bibb or butter lettuce

Simmer broth, tarragon and shallot for 10 minutes. Cover and let steep until cool. Strain (measure and add more broth, if needed to make 2 cups) and return to saucepan. Sprinkle with gelatine and stir over low heat until gelatine is melted. Put a layer in each of 4 small (½ cup size) molds. Chill until firm. Chill rest of aspic until syrupy thick. Dip watercress leaves (or parsley or tarragon) in aspic and place 2 or 3 on set layer in each mold. Chill a few moments, top with egg then cover with rest of aspic. Chill until set, 1 to 2 hours. Unmold on lettuce. Serve with a tarragon-seasoned mayonnaise, if you wish. Makes 4 servings.

Ham and Eggs in Aspic—Make same as above except cover egg with thin slice of ham cut to fit mold. Cover with aspic; chill until firm. Unmold and serve with Mustard Mayonnaise*.

Jellied Eggs with Tongue—Decorate jelly layer in bottom of each mold with two crossed julienne strips pimiento. Chill. Add 2 tablespoons diced pimiento to the syrupy aspic. Set egg on jelly layer; cover with pimiento aspic. Top with slice of tongue, more aspic and chill until set.

Eggs in Aspic Provençal—Make aspic as in Eggs en Gelée,* using consommé madrilène as liquid. Decorate jelly layer in bottom of mold with a few capers; chill a few moments. Set egg on top and cover with aspic. Chill until set and top with two crossed anchovy fillets. Cover with aspic and chill until set.

PAPAYA AND PROSCIUTTO

Hawaii's Kahala Hilton serves this appetizer, and we think it's a cool idea. If, however, papayas aren't aired into your area and prosciutto isn't possible; don't give up! Try a familiar melon and a dry, spicy sausage.

3 papayas
½ pound prosciutto (Smithfield or Westphalian ham, salami or
    cervelat sausage)
3 to 4 limes

Cut papayas in half; remove seeds. Peel and slice each half in 6 slender segments, lengthwise, like peaches. Wrap in saran film and chill 4 hours or until needed. Alternate 6 papaya slices with very

Plate No. 1—Appetizers three ways cool!—Salt-bathed Chinese-Hawaiian *Pineapple Pupus* (p. 22), contrasty *Papaya and Prosciutto* with fresh lime and pepper (p. 34) and *Crudités with Tapenade* (p. 22), the French way with raw vegetables and a lively dip. Photograph courtesy of Calavo.

thinly sliced ham on individual salad plates. Add one or two lime wedges. A pepper mill should be passed at the table. Makes 6 servings.

THE MYSTIQUE OF PATES

What's a pâté? And what's a terrine? Both questions are often asked. Pâté is the French word for pie, and in the strictest sense, consists of a filling of meats, fish, vegetables or fruits baked in a pastry case. By common usage, however, any of the typical savory mixtures of meat or fish baked in a dish called a terrine is a pâté or terrine whether it's lined with pastry, strips of pork fat or baked with no lining at all. Logically, the pâtés, especially those baked in pastry —pâté en croûte—may be served hot or cold. But the terrine is always served cold. Why? As the French say, with a Gallic shrug, "It's the custom."

Practically every village or restaurant in France has its own *pâté maison* or house specialty. Conversely in America, pâtés are featured only by restaurants who serve French or international foods and so our exposure to such foods is more limited. A well-seasoned mixture of ground cooked meats, often of chicken livers or other livers, served with toast or crackers as a cocktail spread is more typical of our concept. Mighty good eating too. But since we've included several recipes for traditional pâtés and terrines as well as some of the delicious quick variety, we might as well set the record straight about which is which.

The Makings of a Good Pâté or terrine are not cheap. Strips of game or poultry, ham or veal are often marinated in cognac, Madeira or other wines before being ground or they may be left in strips to make a patterned dish or one not so smooth and fine in texture. The forcemeat or stuffing that holds these together requires fresh pork and pork fat to keep the loaf moist and sweet, often some ground livers for richness and smooth texture, a quantity of veal for lightness and its gelatinous content. Spices and herbs are added, and sometimes truffles and foie gras or other livers for accent. It gets to be a pretty heady mixture and takes a bit of time to put together. But none of the steps are difficult—it's just a matter of grinding, careful and expert seasoning, layering the materials in the dish—in truth the whole thing can be an interesting challenge. And you can rest assured, a good pâté, rich yet subtle in its appeal, will be remembered by your guests for a long, long time. So give it a try.

The Traditional Earthenware Terrine, rectangular or oval in shape, gives the dish its name and of course is also used for baking pâtés. Enameled cast iron or heavy pottery casseroles or Pyrex loaf pans make excellent substitutes.

For the Fresh Pork Fat specified as a liner for many of the pâtés and also to be ground with the various meats themselves, Julia Child and Simone Beck, our mentors and guides on this subject, suggest fat from around the fresh pork loin since *back fat* is hard to find in America. Their other suggestion is blanched salt pork or fat bacon strips, simmered in water for 10 minutes, drained and dried.

Serve Pâtés with knife and fork as a first course or as part of the hors d'oeuvres. They also make exciting main dishes for luncheon or supper partnered with marinated vegetables or salad and crusty bread. Most pâtés or terrines will keep from 10 days to 2 weeks in the refrigerator. Pour off the excess meat liquids or jelly that surrounds the loaf and seal out air by covering it with melted pork fat. Freezing changes the texture of these mixtures so most experts do not recommend it.

WALNUT BOURBON PATE

A gelatine pâté of chicken livers, well seasoned, textured with walnuts and spiked with bourbon.

½ pound (1 cup) butter
1 small onion, coarsely chopped
1 pound chicken livers
1½ cups chicken broth
2 tablespoons sweet sherry
½ teaspoon paprika
¼ teaspoon ground allspice
¼ teaspoon ground ginger
½ teaspoon salt
⅛ teaspoon Tabasco sauce

1 clove garlic, crushed
½ cup bourbon
1 envelope unflavored gelatine
1 cup chopped walnuts
Parsley and cherry tomatoes
2 hard-cooked eggs
Pumpernickel bread or crackers

Melt butter; add onion, then chicken livers. Cook 10 minutes, stirring occasionally. Add ¾ cup broth, sherry and seasonings. Continue to cook 5 minutes. Remove from heat; add bourbon. Sprinkle gelatine over remaining ¾ cup broth in saucepan. Dissolve it by heating broth over low heat. Place chicken liver mixture in electric blender. Whizz until smooth. Stir broth and walnuts into blender mixture. Lightly oil a 5- to 6-cup mold. Pour pâté into it; chill 4 hours or overnight. Unmold on an oval or round dish, depending on mold's shape. Garnish with parsley, cherry tomatoes and sliced hard-cooked egg wedges placed around the pâté. Serve it with small slices of pumpernickel bread or crackers.

NEW ORLEANS SHRIMP PATE

From the city where shrimp is shrimp and a favorite beverage is Pernod, here's a seafood spread with the unique flavor of both.

¼ cup Pernod[2]
2 tablespoons lemon juice
1½ teaspoons Dijon mustard
½ teaspoon mace
½ teaspoon salt
¼ teaspoon cayenne pepper

¼ pound (½ cup) softened butter
1 pound cooked, deveined shrimp
Watercress
French bread or crackers

Place first 7 ingredients in blender. Cover and whizz until blended. Reserve a few attractive shrimp for garnishing; add the remaining shrimp to blender mixture. Put in a few at a time and turn blender on and off frequently. Use a rubber spatula to move shrimp into cutting position, also to unclog blades. Remove pâté to an attractive bowl. Cover with saran film and chill 4 hours. Garnish with reserved shrimp and a few sprigs of watercress; offer small slices of French bread or crackers to spread shrimp pâté on.

[2] If you do not care for the subtle licorice flavor of Pernod, you may substitute dry sherry.

LIVER PASTE

Leverpastej

This liver spread is a treasured family recipe and a tradition of Swedish Christmas Eve buffets. Some of the ingredients and flavors make it seem similar to a plebeian cousin . . . liverwurst sausage . . . but it's meant to be the star of a special occasion. It's a scene-stealer and we serve it any time of the year.

3 tablespoons butter	½ cup chopped onion
3 tablespoons flour	(1 medium onion)
1 cup heavy cream	4 or 5 anchovy fillets
2 teaspoons salt	3 or 4 black truffles,†
½ teaspoon pepper	(optional)
½ teaspoon allspice	3 eggs
½ teaspoon marjoram	3 tablespoons dry vermouth
1 pound fresh calf or beef	Cucumber Salad*
liver	Fresh dill or parsley
½ pound fresh pork fat	Rye or pumpernickel bread

Melt butter in saucepan; stir in flour. Gradually add cream, continuously beating with a wire whisk. Slowly raise heat; let mixture boil then remove from heat. Cool it. Whisk seasonings into cream sauce. Preferably, chop liver, fat and onion coarsely and process mixture in three parts in a blender. Add anchovies and truffles during last whizzing. Use cooled cream sauce to thin mixture and a rubber spatula to help distribute and avoid clogging. After each part is puréed, empty it into large bowl. *Alternate method:* Ask butcher to grind liver and pork fat 3 times. At home, combine ground meat with onions, anchovies and truffles; grind again, thin it with sauce as needed. Beat eggs well, stir into liver mixture with vermouth.

Preheat oven to 350 degrees F. Pour pâté mixture into buttered terrine or 1-quart loaf pan. Cover with foil and tie securely around top with string. Set in a shallow baking pan; add hot water to reach halfway up outside of pâté pan. Place in lower half of oven and bake for 1½ hours. Allow 1¾ hours if not using loaf-shaped pan; oval and round terrines require longer. When done, remove from oven, undo string and foil covering. Cool it to room temperature; chill 6 hours or overnight in refrigerator. To serve, invert pan on platter. Surround pâté with Cucumber Salad* (drained), sprigs of dill or parsley and slice to serve with rye or pumpernickel bread.

Note: This pâté will keep well under refrigeration, if properly covered or wrapped (as air-tight as possible) in aluminum foil, for about 10 days. Freezing is not too successful, since it alters the quality.

VEAL AND HAM PATE, MOSAIC

Strips of ham and pistachios layered with ground meat make a pretty mosaic when this is sliced. The flavor is subtly rich but not overpowering.

½ pound lean veal
½ pound lean fresh pork
6 ounces fresh pork fat
½ cup minced onion
2 tablespoons butter
½ cup Madeira or port wine
¾ teaspoon salt
½ teaspoon spice Parisienne†
¼ teaspoon allspice
⅛ teaspoon nutmeg
Freshly ground pepper to
    taste

1 clove garlic, crushed
2 eggs, lightly beaten
3 tablespoons brandy or
    cognac
Thin slices fresh pork fat
    or salt pork (approximately
    6 ounces)
6 ounces smoked ham, cut in
    julienne strips ¼ inch thick
½ cup pistachio nuts

Put veal, pork and pork fat through meat grinder 3 times using finest blade. Mixture must be very fine and smooth. Cook onion in butter until soft and golden, 5 to 10 minutes. Add wine and cook a few minutes, until wine is reduced about half. Add to ground meats in large bowl. With wooden spoon beat in seasonings, garlic, eggs and cognac until mixture is light and creamy. Test seasonings by frying a small patty of the mixture; taste and add more seasonings as needed. Line a 1½-quart rectangular or oval terrine or loaf pan with thin pork fat or salt pork (blanch salt pork first by simmering in water 10 minutes; drain and dry). Pack about one-third of the ground meat in terrine; cover with 3 lengthwise rows of ham strips. Between these place 2 rows pistachios. Add another third of ground meat and top with ham and nuts again. Spread with last of ground meat and cover with pork fat slices. Cover with heavy foil, then a heavy lid. Set in pan containing hot water to one-half the depth of terrine. Bake in moderate (350 degree F.) oven 1½ to 2 hours, or until pâté has shrunk slightly from sides and the bubbling fats are no longer cloudy or pink, but clear and yellow. Remove terrine from oven, lift off lid and set a pan or dish on the foil that will fit snugly inside the terrine. Fill pan with heavy object (some canned foods perhaps) to compress the pâté and ensure a smooth, bubble-free texture. Cool several hours, then refrigerate overnight, still weighted down. Cut in slices from the terrine and serve on small plates with fork and knife, French bread or crisp toast and butter if you wish. Makes 24 slices about ⅓ inch thick.

PATE EN GELEE

A pretty way to serve your pâté particularly if the cooking dish or mold is not one of the handsome classic types that goes directly to the table.

Make 3 cups Crystal Aspic* with meat or chicken stock and flavor with a spoonful or two of Madeira or port. Chill until syrupy thick. Remove pâté from dish and trim off fat layer. Wash the terrine and pour in a thin layer of aspic. Decorate with truffle or ripe olive cutouts and chill until set. Return pâté to dish. Pour thickened aspic around it and on top. Chill until set. Unmold and garnish with shiny ripe olives and fancy aspic shapes if you like.

CHAPTER III

Soups ⌒

Reams have been written about the worth of good hot soup. And we're inclined to agree with much of this praise. But, in this book, cold soup is the "in" thing. The idea may be so strange to a number of us and so different from the bracing stimuli of hot soup, it might be necessary to adjust our mental taste reflexes to the delicacy, the soothing quiet effect of chilled soup.

We haven't been able to pinpoint who made the first cold soup, nor where, but notable examples of this refreshment are to be found in many countries. And contrary to what you might think at first, just about as many are from cold lands as from the tropics or sun countries. Russia makes a meaty hot borsch, but their chilled beet borsch is much more popular and more of a classic. The Danes dote on chilled buttermilk soups, and all Scandinavians and Finns as well enjoy their cold fruit soups as a first course or dessert.

Around the Mediterranean, the Greeks make a chilled lemon soup called Avgolemono that looks and tastes like chilled sunshine. The ways to make Spain's iced salad-soup, Gazpacho, are without number. We tried to include the best ones here. Yogurt, buttermilk and interesting herbs and spices such as mint, cardamom, cinnamon, fennel, etc., enhance the cool soups of the Middle East. Tropical countries all over use their lush produce to make exotic cold soups of avocado, coconut, melon, strange vegetables and fish of all kinds.

Perhaps the all-time favorite cold soup is our own American-made original Crème Vichyssoise Glacée created by the late Chef Louis Diat at the New York Ritz. It was named for his hometown, Vichy, France, and was, of course, simply an elegant version of a popular French country potage made of leeks and potatoes.

In like manner, we've found that many of the lovely rich shellfish bisques, the creamy vegetable and chicken soups so beloved by the great chefs, are equally good, or better, served cold. They seem more delicate, and refresh in a quiet, serene sort of way. This chapter is also crammed with ideas for clear cold soups—jellied consommés and madrilènes, consommé—simple or jazzed, spiked with wine, vodka, bourbon and topped with beautiful garnishments to delight the eye.

Our friend the electric blender has worked overtime on most of these soups, as have all of the conveniences and aids needed in contemporary cooking such as canned bouillons and consommés, broths, bouillon cubes, meat extracts and bases, dried and quick-frozen herbs to supplement fresh ones. And the whole gamut of canned, dehydrated and frozen soups we've employed often as quick starters and bases for more elegant cold concoctions.

BLOODY MARY SOUP

Created as a dodge for New York's Sunday morning liquor laws, this zesty, pick-me-upper has become very popular on the brunch menu at the Rainbow Room.

1 medium onion, diced	2 teaspoons Worchestershire
3 stalks celery, diced	sauce
2 tablespoons butter	1 teaspoon salt
2 tablespoons tomato purée	¼ teaspoon pepper
1 tablespoon sugar	1 tablespoon lemon juice
5 cups tomato juice	½ cup vodka

Sauté onion and celery in butter until limp and golden. Add purée and sugar. Cook 1 minute. Add tomato juice and simmer 8 minutes. Add remaining ingredients and strain. Return to heat and bring to boil. Remove and cool. Refrigerate 4 hours or more. Serve in well-chilled, salt-rimmed low highball glasses. Makes 6 servings.

JELLIED CUCUMBER SOUP

A pale green soup, flecked with dill, parsley and pimiento. Peppery seasonings give it a little nip.

1½ envelopes
(1½ tablespoons) unflavored gelatine
3 cans (10½ ounces each) chicken broth
½ cup minced onion
½ teaspoon salt
1 teaspoon finely chopped fresh dill or ¼ teaspoon dry dill weed, crushed
3 tablespoons lemon juice
½ teaspoon Worcestershire sauce
Dash Tabasco
Pepper to taste
2 medium cucumbers
¼ cup chopped pimiento
2 tablespoons finely chopped parsley
Lemon, sliced in thin wedges

Soften gelatine in ½ cup chicken broth. Simmer remaining broth with onion, salt and dill for 10 minutes. Remove from heat. Stir in softened gelatine, lemon juice, Worcestershire and Tabasco sauces and pepper. Stir until gelatine is thoroughly dissolved. Cool, then chill until soup is syrupy thick. Peel, seed and coarsely grate cucumbers. Stir cucumbers, pimiento and parsley into jellied broth. Refrigerate in soup cups 4 hours or more; or let soup congeal in bowl and spoon it out to serve. Serve with lemon wedges. Makes 6 servings.

SNAPPY JELLIED MADRILENE

A peppery soup designed to start your meal off with a zing.

1 tablespoon unflavored gelatine
1 can (6 ounces) cocktail vegetable juice
1 can (13 ounces) red madrilène consommé
1 can (10 ounces) tomato cocktail[1]
1 tablespoon lemon juice
Thin lemon slices
Chopped parsley

[1] A brand of blended tomato, green chili and onion juices.

Sprinkle gelatine over cocktail vegetable juice in a saucepan. Let stand 5 minutes, until softened. Heat slowly, stirring as gelatine dissolves. When clear pour in consommé, other juices and mix. Cool. Refrigerate in covered container or pour into 13×9×2-inch baking pan and stretch a sheet of saran film over it. Chill 4 hours or more. To serve, rough up soup with fork or cut in cubes if chilled in pan. Place in low highball glasses or bouillon cups. Twist a thin slice of lemon on top and sprinkle with parsley. Makes 4 to 6 servings.

JELLIED MUSHROOM CONSOMME

Mushrooms are so low in calories, only 66 in a pound, this recipe will have a special appeal for diet-conscious guests.

1 pound fresh mushrooms,
  finely chopped
2 cans (10½ ounces each)
  consommé

2 teaspoons Angostura bitters
2 teaspoons lemon juice
Dairy sour cream

Before chopping mushrooms, rinse quickly and blot on paper towels. Add mushrooms to consommé in saucepan. Simmer for 5 minutes. Remove from heat and add bitters and lemon juice. Pour into soup cups and chill 4 hours or more; or let it congeal in bowl and spoon it out to serve. Garnish each serving with a dab of sour cream. Makes 6 servings.

CONSOMME IMPERIAL

Caviar and sour cream top this rosy jellied soup. Impressive, but made in minutes.

2 cans (10½ ounces each)
  consommé
1 cup cocktail vegetable juice
2 teaspoons unflavored gelatine
3 tablespoons vodka
1 tablespoon lemon juice,
  or more

Dairy sour cream
1 tablespoon finely minced
  white onion
Red or black caviar

Pour undiluted consommé and vegetable juice into saucepan; sprinkle gelatine on top. Stir over very low heat until gelatine is melted, about 3 minutes. Add vodka and lemon juice to taste. Chill 4 hours, or until firm. Scoop into bowls and top each serving with a generous blob of sour cream, a bit of onion and caviar. Makes 4 elegant servings.

BELMAR HOTEL'S GAZPACHO

The elegant antique Belmar Hotel in Mazatlán, Mexico, is as popular a meeting place today as it was in Pancho Villa's time. Gazpacho, originally created in southern Spain, has had the same classic durability as the old Belmar. Time has not changed either, except for variations in ingredients and methods . . . as served at the Belmar, Gazpacho has dry white wine and is made with a blender.

½ onion
2 stalks celery
½ cucumber, peeled
½ bell pepper
1 can (1 pound, 12 ounces)
    Italian tomatoes
2 sprigs watercress
2 cups tomato juice

1 cup dry white wine
3 tablespoons olive oil
2 tablespoons lemon juice
3 drops Tabasco sauce
1 teaspoon salt
¼ teaspoon pepper
Lemon, thinly sliced
Parsley, finely chopped

In a blender or vegetable-meat grinder combine first 6 ingredients. Chop or blend coarsely. Add next 7 ingredients and blend. Chill at least 4 hours or overnight. Serve in chilled bouillon cups or low highball glasses. Garnish with lemon and a sprinkle of parsley. Makes 4 to 6 servings.

GAZPACHO GRANADA

Our makeup of the colorful Gazpacho served at the Parador de San Francisco in the exotic gardens of the Alhambra in Granada, Spain.

6 large ripe tomatoes, peeled
1 fresh young cucumber, peeled
½ green sweet pepper, cut in chunks
1 onion, peeled and cut in chunks
1 clove garlic, puréed or minced

¼ cup wine vinegar
¼ cup olive oil
½ teaspoon salt
Freshly ground pepper to taste
1 cup tomato juice
1 cup ice cubes
Minced parsley, green pepper and cucumber for garnish

Place in blender part of the tomatoes, cucumber, green pepper and onion. Whizz only until tomatoes are finely chopped but not puréed. Empty into bowl. Repeat until all vegetables are chopped. Stir in remaining ingredients except garnishes. Cover with saran film and chill 4 hours or more. Serve in chilled bowls with 1 or 2 ice cubes in each bowl. Sprinkle each with a little parsley, green pepper and cucumber. Makes 4 to 6 servings.

HUNGARIAN TOMATO SOUP

When tomatoes are abundant and have their best flavor try this cooler. It's superior made with what the produce trade calls stem-tomatoes, the succulent sweet ones allowed to ripen on the vine.

2 pounds ripe tomatoes (about 4 cups chopped)
½ cup chopped onion
2-inch strip lemon peel
Sprig parsley
2 teaspoons sweet Hungarian paprika
1½ tablespoons sugar, or to taste

1½ teaspoons salt, or to taste
2 cups dry white wine
1 tablespoon lemon juice, or to taste
Dairy sour cream, paprika, lemon wedges

Drop tomatoes in boiling water one-half minute. Peel under running cold water. Chop coarsely. Combine with rest of ingredients except lemon juice, sour cream, paprika garnish and lemon wedges. Cook gently until tomatoes are soft, about 15 minutes. They should still have taste of fresh tomatoes. Place in blender and whizz it on and off for a few seconds, until you have a sort of lumpy purée. Add lemon juice (amount of juice depends on tartness of tomatoes). Chill icy cold. Top each serving generously with sour cream and a dash of paprika. Serve with lemon wedges. Makes 4 to 6 servings.

LOBSTER BUTTERMILK BISQUE

Does this sound strange? Just try it once. It's delightfully cool and light.

1 *pound cooked lobster meat (or crab or shrimp)*
1 *onion, chopped*
2 *tablespoons minced carrot*
1 *tablespoon minced parsley*
2 *tablespoons butter*
1 *teaspoon curry powder, or to taste*
2 *cucumbers, peeled, coarsely chopped*
2 *cups bottled clam broth*
6 *cups chilled buttermilk*
2 *teaspoons salt*
Freshly ground pepper
Lemon juice
Dairy sour cream and paprika or sieved hard-cooked egg yolk

Chop seafood coarsely. Cook onion, carrot and parsley in butter until soft. Add curry powder and cucumber; cook a minute or two longer. Whizz in blender with lobster and clam broth until smooth. Do in two batches if your blender container is small. Pour into bowl or storage container and add buttermilk. Season with salt and pepper. Add lemon juice if needed. Chill at least 4 hours. Top each serving with a blob of sour cream and paprika or sieved hard-cooked egg yolk. Makes 6 to 8 servings.

BUTTERMILK BORSCH

A different version of this classic cold soup. Buttermilk gives it a sweet-sour flavor.

1 cup canned julienne beets, drained
1 cup diced carrots, cooked or canned
1 can (10½ ounces) beef bouillon

1 small onion, grated
1 pint (2 cups) buttermilk
Dairy sour cream
Chives, finely chopped

Place all ingredients, except sour cream and chives, in blender. Whizz for a few minutes until smooth. Refrigerate for 4 hours or more. Garnish with a dab of sour cream and a sprinkle of chives. Makes 6 or more servings.

IRANIAN CUCUMBER MAST

This is the summer soup of the Near East, and understandably so, for both cucumber and mast (yogurt) are refreshing and tart. It's especially delicious when followed by fish.

½ cup peeled, seeded, chopped cucumber
½ teaspoon salt
2 cups plain yogurt
1 clove garlic, crushed
1 tablespoon lemon juice
1 teaspoon grated lemon peel

1 teaspoon finely chopped fresh dill (or ¼ teaspoon dry dill weed, crushed)
1 cup water
1 tablespoon finely chopped mint leaves

Place cucumber in bowl and sprinkle with salt. Place half of yogurt in blender (beating yogurt tends to thin it, so only half of total quantity is used here). To blender add garlic, lemon juice and peel, dill and cucumber. Whizz about 8 seconds. Stir in remaining yogurt and water. Adjust seasoning and chill in refrigerator storage container 4 hours or more. Garnish each portion with a sprinkle of mint.

Note: Cucumber should be apparent in this soup by texture as well as taste, hence it is not blended smooth. Makes 6 servings.

WATERCRESS YOGURT SOUP

Watercress hails from ancient Persia; yogurt from Bulgaria. Here both healthful foods are united to form a distinctive, pungent soup.

1 *chicken bouillon cube*
1 *cup boiling water*
1 *cup chopped onion*
½ *cup minced watercress leaves*

About 1 cup plain yogurt
Salt and pepper to taste
Dill pickle, finely chopped
Lemon peel, grated

Dissolve bouillon cube in hot water. Add onion; simmer until soft. Put through sieve or food mill and add watercress leaves. Simmer, tightly covered, for another 10 minutes. Chill. Just before serving, stir in an equal amount of yogurt (about 1 cup). Correct seasoning. Garnish with chopped dill pickle or grated lemon peel. Makes 4 servings.

AVOCADO MADRILENE

Like a pale green sea with red caviar afloat, this congealed soup is a fanciful starter.

1 *large soft-ripe avocado*
2 *cans (10½ ounces) madrilène consommé*
1 *cup dairy sour cream*
2 *teaspoons grated onion*

1½ *tablespoons lemon juice*
Salt and pepper to taste
½ *teaspoon chili powder*
Green food coloring, optional
1 *small jar red caviar*

Halve, seed and peel avocado. Press through sieve into bowl. Add consommé and sour cream and beat with a rotary beater. Season with onion, lemon juice, salt, pepper and chili powder. Add 1 or 2 drops food coloring. Pour into soup cups and chill about 4 hours until jelled, or let it jell in a bowl and spoon it into soup cups at serving time. The effect can be smooth, or you can "make waves." Garnish each portion with a small spoonful of rinsed red caviar. Makes 6 servings.

VICHYSSOISE GLACEE

This crème de la crème of cold soups is always thought of as French, but it was first made and served in America—by French chef Louis Diat at the New York Hotel Ritz. Its plebeian French antecedent is earthy, thick, Potage Parmentier—good leek and potato soup.

3 to 4 leeks, white part
cleaned and diced
(about ½ cup)
1 onion, coarsely chopped
2 tablespoons butter
4 potatoes, peeled and diced
(3½ to 4 cups)
1 quart water

2 teaspoons salt
1 pint hot milk
1 cup heated light cream
White pepper
Few grains nutmeg
1 cup heavy cream
Chopped chives

Clean leeks thoroughly before dicing by holding under running water to get out all the sand that clings in the tight folds and layers of this vegetable. Add with onion to melted butter in large heavy pot or soup kettle. Cook until soft and golden, but not brown. Add potatoes, water and 1½ teaspoons salt (add rest later as needed). Bring to boil; cook gently until vegetables are very soft. Whirl in blender to a fine, smooth purée (in two batches if necessary) or force through food mill or fine sieve. Return purée to soup pot; add hot milk and light cream. Add a little pepper and nutmeg, more salt if needed. Heat just to simmering, stirring often with wooden spoon. Cool, and blend in heavy cream. Chill thoroughly. Top each serving with chopped chives. Makes 6 to 8 servings.

Weight-Watchers Vichyssoise: This is delicious made with all hot milk, then cooled. Stir in 4 tablespoons cream and chill thoroughly.

ONE-OF-EACH SINGHALESE

Senegalese or Singhalese, whichever you prefer, is a delightful, curry-flavored soup. It's made with one of each ingredient, like a good old-fashioned pound cake, and topped off with good old-fashioned, but edible, nasturtium flower petals . . . a pretty picture.

1 medium-size apple
1 medium-size banana
1 medium-size boiling potato
1 medium-size onion
1 medium-size heart of celery, stalks and leaves
1 pint seasoned chicken broth
1 teaspoon curry powder, or to taste

1 cup cream
1 tablespoon butter
Pepper to taste
1 cup dry white wine
1 cup cooked, diced white chicken meat
Nasturtium flower petals or parsley, finely chopped

Peel and coarsely chop fruits and vegetables. Add to salted, boiling chicken broth and simmer until tender. Purée in blender or force through a sieve. Blend curry powder with cream. Add to puréed mixture with butter and pepper to taste. Stir in wine and chicken. Cool, then refrigerate for 4 hours or more. Garnish with nasturtium flower petals, if you have them in your garden, or finely chopped parsley. Makes 6 servings.

CUCUMBER TARRAGON SOUP

Cucumbers and tarragon are good flavor mates in this suave, delicate soup. Our variation of a French classic.

1 quart rich Chicken Stock*
(homemade or canned)
2 teaspoons dried tarragon
leaves or 2 tablespoons
fresh tarragon
4 cucumbers, peeled, lightly
seeded, diced
4 shallots, peeled and diced or
1 bunch green onions,
chopped

⅓ cup butter or margarine
Salt and few grindings black
pepper
1 tablespoon cornstarch
Few drops lemon juice
½ cup cream
Parsley, tarragon or lemon
twists

Simmer chicken stock and tarragon leaves 5 to 10 minutes. Cook cucumbers and shallots or onion in butter over very low heat until soft but not brown, about 10 minutes. Add half the chicken stock and whizz in blender until smooth. Whizz in rest of stock and return mixture to saucepan. Season very lightly with salt and pepper. Moisten cornstarch with a tablespoon water; stir into soup. Cook until it thickens slightly. Add a few drops lemon juice. Cool slightly and stir in cream. Refrigerate 4 hours or more, to develop flavors. Garnish each serving with a dainty leaf of parsley or fresh tarragon or a thin, thin twist of lemon. Makes 6 servings.

COCONUT CURRY SOUP

This exciting blender-made soup is better made with fresh coconut since the packaged has sugar added, but delicious either way.

2½ cups chicken broth
½ onion, chopped
½ cup chopped celery
1 small potato, diced
¼ bay leaf
½ teaspoon salt, or to taste
Dash ground cloves

1 teaspoon curry powder
1 tablespoon cornstarch
1 cup Coconut Milk*
Cayenne pepper
Snipped chives and toasted
  almond slivers

In saucepan, simmer together broth, vegetables, bay leaf, ½ teaspoon salt and cloves until potato is quite tender, about 10 minutes. Moisten curry powder and cornstarch in a little of the coconut milk; add with rest of coconut milk to broth. Heat to boiling. Season with a few grains cayenne pepper, more salt if needed (it all depends on the broth you use). Cool, cover with saran film and chill 4 hours or more. Sprinkle each serving with a few snipped chives and almond slivers. Makes 4 servings.

COCONUT MILK

Fresh or Fresh Frozen Coconut: Pour 1 cup boiling water over 2 cups grated fresh coconut (¾ cup boiling water over 2 cups fresh frozen coconut). Let stand 20 minutes and strain through double thickness of cheesecloth, pressing to obtain as much creamy pulp as possible.

Packaged Coconut: Combine 1 cup shredded or 1⅓ cups flaked coconut with 1 cup milk; simmer over low heat until mixture foams, about 2 minutes. Cool slightly and strain through double thickness of cheesecloth, pressing out as much creamy pulp as possible.

Blender-made: Place 1 cup flaked or shredded coconut and 1 cup milk in blender container. Blend at high speed at least 40 seconds. Press through fine strainer or double thickness of cheesecloth as above. Refrigerate. Makes 1 cup.

LATIN PUMPKIN SOUP

La Fonda del Sol in New York provided us with the recipe and inspiration for this bisque. Their method is "from scratch" . . . cooking pumpkin and all that . . . ours is a mini-method.

½ cup chopped onion
3 scallions or green onions
2 cans (13¾ ounces each)
  chicken broth
1 can (1 pound) or 2 cups
  cooked, puréed pumpkin
½ teaspoon salt

¼ teaspoon pepper
½ cup light cream
2 medium tomatoes, thinly
  sliced
½ cup unsweetened heavy
  cream, whipped

Simmer onion and sliced white part of scallions (reserve green part) about 5 minutes with 1 can chicken broth. Add and cool it with second can of broth. Empty pumpkin into blender; add broth mixture, and seasoning. Whizz until smooth (in two batches if necessary). (Or press mixture through a fine sieve.) Add cream; whizz again. Check seasoning. Refrigerate until well chilled, 4 hours or more. Pour into bouillon cups. Gently float a thin slice of tomato on each serving. Use elsewhere or discard any remaining pieces of tomato. Garnish with a dab of whipped cream. Sprinkle finely chopped green part of scallions on top. Makes 8 servings.

ICED AVGOLEMONO

Avgolemono, which means egg with lemon, is almost as familiar to tourists in Greece as the Acropolis. This lemony chicken soup, while sometimes served hot, is much more full-flavored when chilled.

3 cups canned condensed
  chicken broth
3 cups water
⅓ cup rice
1 teaspoon salt
3 egg yolks

⅓ cup fresh lemon juice
½ teaspoon monosodium
  glutamate
Lemon wedges
Snipped pimiento

In a large saucepan, bring chicken broth, water, rice and salt to boil. Reduce heat and simmer covered 15 to 20 minutes or until rice is cooked. Remove saucepan from heat. In a bowl beat egg yolks lightly; add lemon juice and monosodium glutamate. With a whisk, add and blend about 2 cups of hot broth into egg-lemon mixture. Gradually pour this mixture back into rest of soup. Whisk or beat until soup has thickened very slightly. Cool; then refrigerate 4 hours or more. Skim if you wish before serving, and stir thoroughly. Serve in chilled bouillon cups or soup bowls. Garnish with lemon wedges and scatter a few snips of pimiento over each portion. Makes 6 to 8 servings.

Note: For a delicious sauce on meats, fish and vegetables the method is the same, just reduce the broth and water to 1½ cups each and strain to remove rice.

SHRIMP CUCUMBER BISQUE

If you like cucumbers, you will love this soup: It is lightly flavored and textured with specks of cucumbers and shrimp.

3 medium cucumbers	1 cup cream
3 tablespoons butter	1½ tablespoons lemon juice
1 medium-size leek	1 tablespoon finely chopped
2 bay leaves	mint or parsley
1½ tablespoons flour	⅔ cup finely chopped cooked
3 cups chicken broth	or canned shrimp
1 teaspoon salt	Dairy sour cream

Peel cucumbers; slice 2 and reserve one. Melt butter in skillet; add sliced cucumbers, sliced white part only of leek and bay leaves. Cover and steam over low heat until softened, about 20 minutes. Remove bay leaves. Blend in flour and chicken broth. Cook and stir until lightly thickened. Season with salt. Purée in blender or press through sieve. Pour into refrigerator storage container and chill 4 hours or more. Seed and grate remaining cucumber. Stir it into chilled soup with cream, lemon juice, mint or parsley and chopped shrimp. Check seasoning. Serve in chilled cups with a dab of sour cream on top of each portion. Makes 6 servings.

ICED AVOCADO CLAM SOUP

An unbeatable combination—sea-tangy clams and creamy avocado—in a cool green soup you can make in minutes.

1 soft-ripe avocado (about 1 cup diced)	½ cup cream
	Salt, nutmeg, Tabasco
1 can (10½ ounces) cream of chicken soup	Lemon juice
	Green food coloring, if needed
1 cup milk	
1 can (7¼ to 10½ ounces) minced or chopped clams	Salted whipped cream puffs and grated lemon peel

Halve, seed, peel and dice avocado. Combine with soup, milk, clams and juice. Whizz in blender (in two batches if necessary) until smooth. Blend in cream, seasonings and lemon juice to taste. Tint a soft pale green with few drops coloring if needed. Chill. Thin with more milk or cream to a pleasing consistency if it thickens after being chilled. Serve in chilled bowls. Top each with puff of salted whipped cream sprinkled with grated lemon peel. Makes 4 servings.

COLD CRAB GUMBO

It has been said that Robert Benchley, while discussing one of his favorite topics—food—remarked, "The real test of good hot food is if it tastes as good cold." Proof of his truism is that gumbo, traditionally served hot, is the most popular cold soup on the Chicago Club menu.

½ cup diced onion	1 cup canned cut okra
½ cup diced celery	1 bay leaf
½ cup diced green pepper	1 teaspoon salt
½ cup diced leeks	¼ teaspoon pepper
2 tablespoons butter	1 package (8 ounces) frozen crab meat, defrosted and drained or 1 can (7½ ounces) crab meat, drained
1 quart chicken broth	
1 cup or 1 can (8¾ ounces) chopped stewed tomatoes	

Cook first 4 vegetables in butter until limp. Add broth, tomatoes, okra and bay leaf. Season with salt and pepper. Simmer about 40 minutes. Cool, uncovered. Refrigerate in a wide-mouthed container. After fat has risen as a solid layer, skim it off. Before serving, stir in crab meat.

Soup should be served very cold; a few minutes in a freezer will improve it. You may want to pass a bottle of Louisiana hot sauce or Tabasco sauce for guests to add, if desired. Makes 6 to 8 servings.

PINK STRAWBERRY SOUP

From the Rainbow Room, atop New York's Rockefeller Center, a rainbow of a soup that packs a punch with its "broth" of port wine.

3 tablespoons cornstarch
1 cup cold water
⅘ quart (24 ounces) port
 wine
1 pint (2 cups) fresh
 strawberries

¼ cup sugar
Pinch salt
2 to 3 tablespoons lemon
 juice, to taste
Light cream

Blend cornstarch with water in medium saucepan. Add ½ bottle of wine; bring to boil. Lower heat and simmer 5 minutes; stirring often. Measure whole or cut strawberries (halve or quarter large ones) and add to saucepan ingredients. Add sugar, salt, remaining ½ bottle wine and stir to blend. Remove from heat and add lemon juice to taste. Cool, then chill 4 hours or more. This soup is most effective served in low highball glasses or bouillon cups. Serve with cream. It may be a first or last course. Makes 6 servings.

BLUEBERRY WINE SOUP

As either a first or last course, this soup is a conversation piece. Grape and pineapple juice, wine, stick cinnamon and blueberries produce such a delectable ambrosia when combined, it belies description.

3 tablespoons quick-cooking tapioca
1½ cups boiling water
2 cups grape juice
2 cups pineapple juice
½ cup sugar
Peel of 1 lemon, finely grated

1 piece (2 inches) stick cinnamon
½ cup dry sherry
1 cup fresh blueberries (or unsweetened, frozen blueberries)
Dairy sour cream

Stir tapioca into rapidly boiling water. Stir often and cook until clear. Add grape and pineapple juice, bring to a boil. Add sugar, lemon peel and cinnamon. Cook over low heat for 10 minutes. Remove from heat and add sherry and blueberries. Cool, then refrigerate 4 hours or more. Garnish each portion with a dab of sour cream. Makes 6 servings.

PEACHES 'N' CREAM SOUP

Try this blender-easy, Scandinavian-influenced soup as your first or last course . . . it's peachy keen!

1 package (12 ounces) frozen
   peaches
1½ cups cold milk
3 tablespoons instant vanilla
   pudding mix

¼ teaspoon almond extract
Blanched sliced or slivered
   almonds

Defrost peaches sufficiently to remove from package. Empty into bowl and cut into bite-size chunks with sharp knife. Pour into blender. Add other ingredients except almonds, cover and whizz on high speed until liquified. Serve immediately in chilled bouillon cups. If made ahead, chill a few minutes in freezer and stir well. Float a few almond pieces on each portion. Makes 3 to 4 servings. If more servings are desired, double amounts and process ingredients in two batches in blender.

CHAPTER IV

Entrées ❧

Fish, Poultry, Meats, Eggs

One of the most appealing features of a cold entrée is its beauty and stay-put qualities. Often you can make it hours ahead, or even days, decorate it artfully with fresh herb leaves, truffles, pimiento, gay strips of lemon peel, then cover it with a film of transparent aspic. It will look exactly the same when you present it to your guests. There's no last-minute cooking or beating or heating, no remembering to season, no thickening of sauces or adding of butter or cream. Simply pull from the refrigerator and serve.

We call our cold dishes the "ready foods" and they truly are that. You make them in your own time, more or less at your own pace. We admit some of the steps in cooking a number of the classic recipes—cooling and de-greasing stock for an aspic, clarifying the aspic, glazing, final decorations, and such—all require time. But you can space the various steps pretty well to suit your other activities. And, you don't make such dishes every day. To balance them, we've included dozens of imaginative recipes that are quick and easy, appealing to family and guests alike.

When you think of cold meats, fish and the like, you usually picture an elaborate summer buffet or a beautiful flower-decked warm-weather luncheon. The foods in this chapter are perfect for such occasions, but let's not limit them to a warm season. Cold dishes have been an integral part, and perhaps the handsomest, of our winter holiday buffets and parties since any of us can remember— regal cold roasts of beef, ham and turkey, molded seafoods and fruits, ornate iced desserts and puddings. Not to mention our casual Dutch-lunch spreads of cold ham, tongue, bologna and sausages of all kinds served with mustards, potato salad, dill pickles, rye bread and beer in all seasons. And what would a picnic be without cold ham or meat for sandwiches, or cold fried or roast chicken to enjoy with bread and butter, a cool salad and watermelon or ice cream?

For all these happy occasions then, and many more, the following recipes are intended.

POACHED FISH—THE EPICURE'S WAY

Much as we agree with the French saying, "It's the sauce that makes the fish," we will go beyond that and say, "It is the cooking (or overcooking) that un-makes the fish." Since many famous cold dishes are based on poached fish, it seems appropriate to discuss this cooking method.

Fish itself is tender and delicate, and the gentle simmering in a seasoned liquid preserves and enhances that delicacy. Choose the liquid or court bouillon that best suits the fish itself and the final dish. Recipes for court bouillons are given in the chapter on Know-how for Cold Dishes. A very flavorful fish like red snapper should be cooked in a light, simply flavored liquid, while trout or sole and most shellfish, more delicate and subtle in flavor, need the extra seasonings of herbs and wine in the cooking mixture. Directions for poaching a whole large fish are given in Salmon in Aspic.*

POACHED FISH STEAKS

Steaks or center cuts, 1 to 1½ inches thick from salmon, halibut, cod and other such firm fish are best. In wide pan or skillet, heat just enough of the selected court bouillon barely to cover fish. Place fish on buttered trivet or rack (or tie loosely in cheesecloth leaving long ends for handles). Lower into simmering liquid and cook gently without allowing the water even to bubble—it should just almost smile, but never break the surface. Steaks require 8 to 12 minutes, depending on thickness. The flesh will look opaque, but moist, and may be pierced easily with a fork. If fish is overcooked and separates completely into flakes, it will be dry and rather tasteless. (Incidentally, this overcooking of fish is exactly the reason many persons do not appreciate and enjoy poached fish—they never taste it at its best.) Drain fish and save liquid if needed for a sauce or aspic. It continues to cook if left in the hot liquid. Cool, then cover with saran film and chill. Serve with one of the mayonnaise sauces found in the Sauces chapter, or complete as directed in specific recipes.

POACHED FISH FILLETS

If possible, choose thick, meaty firm fillets of sole, turbot, trout, snapper, bluefish, sea bass, redfish, cod, ocean perch and the like. It's best to fold thin fillets in half as they are fragile and break up easily in poaching. Butter a heat-proof, shallow dish or pan and sprinkle lightly with chopped parsley and green onions or shallots. Lay fillets, slightly overlapping, in pan and pour in enough selected cold court bouillon barely to cover. Cover pan loosely with buttered brown paper and heat on top of stove until liquid almost simmers. Place in moderate oven (350 degrees F.) for 6 to 10 minutes, depending on thickness of fish, or until fish is opaque, but moist-looking. Drain and cool, saving liquid for sauce or aspic. If desired, fillets may be poached on top, directly over heat, but the liquid is more apt to bubble and result in overcooked fillets that fall apart.

Trout and other whole small fish are poached the same as fillets.

MASKED FISH FILLETS

An easy way to make a showy luncheon platter. Poach and chill 2 pounds thick, firm, light-fleshed fish fillets as above. Arrange on platter attractively, petal style or in neat symmetrical rows, and spread each with desired mayonnaise sauce to mask completely. Keep shapes of fillets defined. Decorate each according to the fish and its sauce.

*For Caper Mayonnaise.** Top each masked fillet with a row of capers separated with thin slivers of pimiento. Garnish plate with frilly escarole or chicory and quartered, hard-cooked eggs.

*For Dill Cream Mayonnaise.** Top each masked fillet with a feathery spray of fresh dill. Ring plate with lemon slices slashed halfway through, then twisted airily.

*For Sauce Verte.** Top each masked fillet with row of pimiento-stuffed olive slices and decorate platter with small sprigs of watercress. Two pounds fillets make 4 to 6 servings.

HALIBUT WITH MAYONNAISE RUSSE

The myriad ways to serve poached fish are limited only by the fish available in your area and your own imagination. This is an elegant contrast in flavors and suitable for one of your special occasions.

Poach 4 thick halibut steaks by basic directions for Poached Fish Steaks.* Cool fish with a few spoonfuls of court bouillon poured over them. Cover and chill. Make Mayonnaise Russe* and chill. Arrange steaks attractively on platter and circle with overlapping slices of thinly sliced lemon and a few sprays of watercress. Top each steak with a spoonful of the mayonnaise and serve rest in a sauce bowl. Makes 4 servings.

MAYONNAISE RUSSE

1 cup mayonnaise
1 tablespoon fresh lemon
   juice
1 tablespoon minced onion

1 teaspoon grated lemon peel
2 tablespoons cream
1 to 2 tablespoons black
   caviar

Blend all ingredients, gently swirling in the caviar last. Cover and chill. Makes 1¼ cups.

SALMON IN ASPIC

What could be more spectacular for a party buffet than a magnificent whole salmon glazed in a shiny clear aspic, fancifully decorated, and served in a sea of sparkling chopped aspic? If you don't have a long French fish poacher, a big old-fashioned turkey roaster is perfect. Or simpler still, try this neat trick we figured out. Cut a large fish in halves, steam-poach it in the oven in your meat roasting pan and reassemble to glaze and serve.

6 to 8 pound whole salmon
About 2½ quarts White
   Wine Court Bouillon*
1½ quarts Fish Aspic Glaze*
Green and blue food coloring

2 cucumbers, sliced paper
   thin
Watercress or sprays fresh dill
Lemon slices
Dill Cream Mayonnaise*

Cut fish in halves crosswise on a slight diagonal. Leave head and tail intact, if possible. Tie each half in cheesecloth leaving long ends for handles. Place in large meat roasting pan (15×10×2½ inches is perfect). Pour in boiling hot court bouillon to half fill pan; seal pan with foil. Steam-poach in oven at 350 degrees F. 6 to 8 minutes per pound, until flesh looks opaque, but moist, and flakes when pierced with tip of knife. Cool fish in liquid; lift onto board and unwrap carefully. (Use liquid in making fish aspic glaze.) Peel off skin between head and tail and gently scrape off grayish fat layer to expose pretty pink salmon flesh. Wrap halves in saran film and chill. Reassemble on platter as whole fish. Measure 2 cups fish aspic glaze into small bowl and set in bowl of ice cubes until syrupy thick. Tint rest of aspic a pale seafoamy green with about 3 drops green food coloring, 1 drop of blue. Pour into shallow pan and chill until firm to use as garnish. Coat fish evenly with a thin layer of the syrupy glaze (keep it syrupy by setting bowl in either warm water or ice cubes as necessary). Decorate midsection of fish with neat row of cucumber slices; chill till set in place just a few minutes. Spoon rest of syrupy glaze over fish to coat evenly. Chill. At serving time chop tinted aspic and tumble onto platter around fish. Decorate with watercress or dill, more slices of cucumber and lemon. Serve with dill cream mayon-

naise. Or you can be very fancy with decorations for this platter—
mingle with the glittery chopped aspic, lemon shells filled with
tiny marinated shrimp, stuffed hard-cooked eggs topped with caviar
or capers, marinated pimiento strips heaped in cucumber boats,
and so on and on. An 8-pound salmon will serve 12 to 15, or
more for a buffet with other dishes.

LOBSTER TAILS FIGARO

Originally created for freshly boiled live lobster, split and stuffed,
this is more practical and effective made with lobster tails, which
are available everywhere, year round, fresh or frozen.

¼ cup white wine vinegar
2 tablespoons salt
Small bay leaf
6 lobster tails (about 6 ounces
  each)
1 teaspoon dried tarragon
  leaves
1 teaspoon dried chervil leaves
1 tablespoon minced green
  onion

1½ tablespoons lemon juice
3 tablespoons chili sauce
1 cup mayonnaise
Green pepper slivers
Crystal Aspic,* optional
Frilly salad greens and
  hard-cooked eggs

Bring to boil in large kettle 2 quarts water, the vinegar, salt, bay
leaf. (Or use about 2 quarts White Wine Court Bouillon,* if you
prefer.) Add lobster; bring to boil again, then simmer 6 minutes.
Cool in liquid. With kitchen shears, cut along sides of soft undershell
and lift it out. Carefully pull out lobster meat in one piece; dry
shells and set aside. Slice three attractive crosswise slices or medallions
from center of each tail for decoration; dice remainder. Mix tarragon,
chervil, onion, lemon juice and chili sauce with mayonnaise and
blend about ½ cup into lobster. Pack into shells. Top each with 3
lobster medallions separated with thin slivers of green pepper. If
you like, cover with a thin film of almost-set crystal aspic. Chill until
set. At serving time, arrange lobster tails in neat symmetrical row
or petal style on chilled plate. Garnish with crisp greens and
quartered hard-cooked eggs. Serve rest of dressing separately. Makes
6 servings.

BEERY GOOD SHRIMP

Beer and special seasonings make the difference in these spicy tender shrimp. Great for any informal get-together—with French bread and beer.

3 cans (12 ounces each) beer
1 bay leaf
3 dried, hot red chili peppers
8 whole cloves
1 teaspoon fennel or anise
    seeds (or ½ teaspoon each
    dried thyme and tarragon
    leaves, if the licorice tang of
    anise is not enjoyed)

2 pounds jumbo shrimp,
    in-the-shell
1½ teaspoons salt, or to taste
Crushed ice
Sprigs of greenery
Diable Dressing*

Combine in large kettle, all ingredients except shrimp, salt, ice and dressing. Bring to boil and simmer about 5 minutes. Add shrimp; bring to full boil. Reduce heat immediately and simmer 4 to 5 minutes. Add salt. Cool a few minutes. Skim shrimp from liquid; remove shells and dark vein leaving tails intact. Return shrimp to liquid and refrigerate several hours. Drain and heap in glass bowl banked with crushed ice. Garnish with sprigs of greenery. Serve with diable dressing. Makes 6 to 8 servings.

Note: For calorie watchers, the shrimp are delectable with no sauce at all.

Diable Dressing

Devilishly spicy and lusty as the shrimp themselves.

1 cup mayonnaise
1 cup dairy sour cream
½ cup catsup
1 small clove garlic, crushed
1½ tablespoons
    Worcestershire sauce

2 tablespoons lemon juice
Tabasco sauce to taste
Chives

Mix all ingredients but chives; chill. Top with chives. Makes about 2½ cups.

SNOWY SEA ASPIC

For a change, we've added a bit of mayonnaise to the clear aspic base of this fish and shellfish combination. Enough to make the mold look snowy white and cool, yet not enough to change its lightness.

½ pound white-meat fish fillets

3 cups Quick Chicken or Fish Stock*

2 envelopes unflavored gelatine

½ cup dry white wine or sherry

Salt and lemon juice, if needed

⅓ cup mayonnaise

1 cup cooked, deveined shrimp

1 cup cooked lobster or crab meat

Thin lemon slices, halved

Cook fish fillets in chicken or fish stock by basic directions for Poached Fish Fillets.* Drain and cool. Strain stock; measure again for 3 cups. Sprinkle gelatine over wine and add to hot stock. Stir over low heat until completely dissolved. Taste and add salt and lemon juice if needed. Chill until syrupy thick. Flake cooled fillets (you should have about 1 cup). Fold mayonnaise into aspic, then gently fold in fish flakes and shellfish. Turn into 6-cup fish-shaped or other mold and chill until set, 4 hours or more. Unmold on chilled platter and ring with lemon slices. Makes 6 servings. Serve with hot biscuits and a platter of sliced tomatoes.

PRINCESS CRAB MOUSSE

A creamy pink concoction, delicious and cool. Ideal for a fancy luncheon.

1 pound frozen King crab meat, defrosted (or about 3 cups fresh or canned crab meat)

2 cups bottled clam juice (part or all may be chicken broth)

2 onion slices

1 carrot, sliced

2 lemon slices

½ teaspoon each dried tarragon and marjoram

2 envelopes unflavored gelatine

Cayenne pepper

¼ teaspoon nutmeg

1 tablespoon lemon juice

Salt

1 cup heavy cream

¼ cup mayonnaise

Curly endive (chicory) or watercress

Crab legs or big pieces for garnish

Lemon twists

(King crab meat was chosen for this because of its pretty pink color and general availability. Other crab may be used.) Pick over crab; remove any bits of shell. Simmer together for about 10 minutes the clam juice, onion, carrot, lemon, herbs tied in cheesecloth. Remove herbs and lemon. Soften gelatine in ½ cup cold water; dissolve in the hot clam liquid. Add crab meat. In two portions, pour into blender and whizz until smooth (or chop crab very fine and force clam juice and vegetables through food mill or sieve). Combine and season to taste, on the plus side, with cayenne and nutmeg. Add lemon juice, and salt if needed. It should be delicate, but well seasoned for whipped cream added later will bland it. Chill crab mixture until thick and heavy, but not set. Whip cream until thick and softly peaked, but not stiff and dry. Gently fold mayonnaise and cream into crab. Pour into 6-cup mold and chill until firm, 4 hours or more. Unmold onto a pretty glass plate and decorate with frilly greens, crab legs and thin slices lemon slashed half through and twisted. Makes 12 or more servings. Croissants or other light crisp rolls are nice with this, also a chilled vegetable and melon in season.

CRAB MOUSSE IN ASPIC

Make 4 cups Crystal Aspic* and pour 2 cups of it into shallow pan.
Chill firm to use as garnish. With remaining 2 cups aspic, line and
decorate 2-quart mold as described in To Line a Mold with Aspic.*
Chill until sticky firm and carefully fill with Princess Crab Mousse.*
Chill until firm, 6 hours or overnight. Unmold on chilled platter.
Chop garnish aspic coarsely and heap around mousse. Decorate with
gay twists of lemon and sprigs of dill.

SHRIMP MOUSSE EN GELEE

Pink shrimp mousse sparkles in a sheath of clear aspic. A real party
maker.

3 envelopes unflavored
    gelatine
3 cups cold Clarified Chicken
    Stock*
Lemon juice
Salt and monosodium
    glutamate
1½ teaspoons dried dill or
    1 tablespoon chopped
    fresh dill
½ teaspoon spice Parisienne†

1 can (10 ounces)
    frozen cream of shrimp
    soup, defrosted
3 cups deveined, cooked
    shrimp
2 tablespoons minced green
    onion
Tabasco sauce
Red food coloring, if needed
½ cup dairy sour cream
1 cup heavy cream, whipped

For clear aspic layer, sprinkle 1 envelope gelatine over 2 cups stock;
stir over low heat until gelatine melts and liquid is clear. Season
rather sharply with about 2 tablespoons lemon juice, a little salt
and monosodium glutamate. Strain through several layers wet cheesecloth. Chill until syrupy thick. For mousse, sprinkle 2 envelopes
gelatine over remaining 1 cup cold stock; stir over low heat until
gelatine melts. Add dill, spice, shrimp soup and 2½ cups shrimp.
Whizz in blender until smooth (in two batches if necessary). Add
green onion, Tabasco and lemon juice and salt to taste. If mixture
is pale, tint a pretty shrimp pink with few drops red coloring

as cream will pale it. Chill until thick but not set. Line 6- to 7-cup fish-shaped or other mold with the clear aspic as described in To Line a Mold with Aspic.* If you wish, decorate aspic layer with thin lengthwise slices shrimp or green pepper crescents cut with small truffle cutter and arranged to look like fish scales. Gently fold sour cream and whipped cream into mousse. Spoon carefully over sticky firm aspic layer. Cover with saran film and chill until firm, 4 hours or overnight. Unmold and decorate with fresh dill and chilled shrimp. It's also pretty with fish Crystal Aspic* finely chopped and tumbled onto platter around mousse. Makes 8 or more servings.

Chicken Mousse—Substitute 2½ cups cooked chicken for shrimp, cream of chicken soup for shrimp soup in recipe above. Add ½ cup diced avocado and 1 tablespoon curry powder. Omit dill. Decorate aspic layer in bottom *only* of mold with thin crescents of avocado and slices of hard-cooked egg.

Lobster Mousse—Substitute 2½ cups cooked lobster meat for shrimp in recipe above. Add 1 teaspoon each tarragon and chervil. Omit dill. Use 1 cup each bottled clam juice and tomato juice for the clear aspic layer. Decorate platter with chopped aspic and cucumber twists.

RITZY SALMON

Looks elegant, tastes great and is easy.

3 cans (7¾ ounces each) red salmon

3 cups peeled, thinly sliced cucumber

Salt

6 hard-cooked eggs

2 tablespoons soft butter

2 tablespoons Dijon mustard†

2 teaspoons plus 1 tablespoon minced green onion

¾ cup mayonnaise

½ cup dairy sour cream

1 tablespoon minced parsley

1 tablespoon chopped fresh dill or 1 teaspoon dried dill

2 tablespoons lemon juice

Bibb lettuce

Red caviar

Lemon wedges

Refrigerate salmon in can overnight. Sprinkle cucumber with a little salt; let stand 30 minutes. Rinse, drain and chill. Halve eggs lengthwise; mash yolks with butter, a little salt, 1 tablespoon mustard, 2 teaspoons minced onion and 1 to 2 tablespoons of the mayonnaise. Refill whites; cover with saran film and chill. Mix remaining mayonnaise, sour cream, remaining mustard, parsley, dill, lemon juice and 1 tablespoon onion. Chill. Outline platter with lettuce leaves; cover with drained cucumbers leaving center free for salmon. Open salmon and gently ease out of can onto paper toweling to drain. Lift carefully with wide spatula to platter keeping salmon in original shape. Pour part of dressing over salmon; serve rest separately. Top eggs with a little red caviar; arrange on platter with lemon wedges. Makes 6 servings.

CHICKEN IN SNOW

While the Crosby "Bobcat" orchestra was touring the South doing one-night stands, this became a family favorite. It's a gently simmered chicken, boned and then blanketed in a pale, creamy sauce flavored with a bouquet of mace and lemon.

1 (3 to 4 pounds) roasting chicken, cut up
2½ cups chicken broth
3 whole carrots
4 stalks celery
4 small onions
1 cup heavy cream
Peel ½ lemon
2 tablespoons butter

1½ tablespoons flour
¼ teaspoon salt
⅛ teaspoon white pepper
¼ teaspoon powdered mace
2 tablespoons lemon juice
2 to 3 strips bacon, cut crosswise in half
Parsley

Place chicken in deep pot and cover with broth. Add carrots, celery and onions. Cover and simmer gently for about 1 hour, until quite tender. Remove from heat and cool in broth. Take chicken from pot and remove skin. Reserve broth. Also save carrots to use in garnishing later. Bone chicken in as large and attractive pieces as possible. Arrange on platter with white meat in center, dark pieces around edges. Prepare cream sauce. In top of double boiler, heat cream with lemon peel. In a pan melt butter and blend in flour. Add a little hot cream gradually, stir to blend. Return to double boiler; add ½ cup strained chicken broth (sauce thickens more as it cools). Cook 15 minutes. (Save remaining broth for soups, aspics, gravies, etc.) Remove lemon peel from sauce; add salt, pepper, mace and lemon juice. Pour sauce over chicken carefully, evenly coating each piece. Cool a few minutes. Slice carrots round or julienne and distribute around chicken. Cover with a self-supporting inverted baking dish (to cover the food, yet not spoil the appearance of the sauce). Place in refrigerator 4 hours to chill thoroughly. Before serving, fry bacon crisply and while cooking train each piece into a curl; drain on paper. Garnish platter with bacon and parsley flowerets. Makes 4 to 6 servings.

CHICKEN WITH GINGER SAUCE
Chung Yau Kai

Freshly grated ginger root is the vital element in this Chinese-Hawaiian recipe. It gives a pungent, aromatic savor to simple cold chicken.

1 tablespoon salt
1 (1 inch) slice fresh ginger root,† peeled
1 (3 to 4 pounds) roasting chicken

Sauce:

¾ cup salad oil
½ teaspoon salt
¼ teaspoon monosodium glutamate
¼ cup lemon juice
1 clove garlic, crushed

¼ cup grated fresh ginger root
½ cup (1-inch slivers) green onion
Chinese parsley (cilantro),† optional

Bring 2 quarts water, 1 tablespoon salt and slice of ginger to boil. Add whole chicken; cover and immediately turn to lowest heat for 25 minutes. Turn chicken; cover and let stand at lowest heat, barely simmering, another 25 minutes. Remove from broth; rinse quickly in cold water; drain. (Reserve broth for another use.) Remove skin and bones from chicken. Place chicken in flat serving bowl; cover and chill. For sauce, heat oil with salt, monosodium glutamate; stir to dissolve. Cool and add lemon juice, garlic and ginger. Beat with fork; add onion and pour over chicken. Garnish with chopped Chinese parsley if it's available. Serve with rice and perhaps a pickled vegetable. Makes 4 to 6 servings.

CHINESE CHICKEN SALAD

Sow See Gai

This Cantonese banquet dish, which means hand-shredded chicken, is a whopper to make but worth it. All ingredients are available in supermarkets or Chinese specialty stores. The transparent bean threads are fun; they expand greatly and startlingly when cooked, and look like some kind of styrofoam wiring. Then they shrink unbelievably when combined with the chicken dressing.

1 (2½ pounds) boiler-fryer
    chicken
Salt
¼ cup soy sauce
¼ cup dry sherry or sake†
½ teaspoon fresh ginger juice
    (pressed through garlic press)
    or grated fresh ginger root†

2 tablespoons honey
Cooking oil for deep-frying
    (about 2 quarts)
½ (7¾ ounces) package bean
    threads (Saifun)†
1 tablespoon (or more) white
    or black seasame seeds†

Salad Dressing:

½ teaspoon Chinese salt[1]
½ teaspoon sugar
¼ teaspoon dry mustard
2 tablespoons soy sauce
2 tablespoons dry sherry
    or sake†

Juice of 1 lemon
2 tablespoons peanut or salad
    oil, heated to boiling
½ teaspoon sesame oil†
White pepper to taste

[1] Chinese salt (Wah Yeem) is made by frying ⅔ part table salt with ⅓ part Chinese 5-Spice† seasoning. If Chinese 5-Spice is unavailable, substitute with cinnamon or equal parts cinnamon, allspice and ground anise.

Salad Ingredients:

⅓ cup chopped coriander
  leaves†

4 green onions, slivered
  in 2- to 3-inch lengths

2 or more cups shredded
  lettuce

Virginia ham or prosciutto,
  optional

Rub inside of cleaned chicken with salt. Marinate 1 hour or longer in mixture of ¼ cup soy sauce, ¼ cup wine, ginger and honey. In the Chinese manner, deep-fry whole chicken in oil heated to 350 degrees F. Frying whole prevents loss of juices. Fry 15 to 20 minutes on each side, until skin breaks at joints. The skin turns quite brown while cooking; it may be discarded. When chicken is tender, drain on brown paper and cool. Do not discard cooking oil. Shred meat with fingers; set aside and cover with saran film to prevent drying. Refrigerate. With sharp kitchen shears, cut bean threads in 2- to 3-inch lengths (they are almost impossible to break up by hand). Deep-fry IN VERY SMALL quantities. As they expand, they are done. Remove; drain on brown paper and set aside. If preparing recipe a day ahead, place bean threads in large brown paper bag to store. In a small skillet toast sesame seeds using a teaspoon or more of oil.

Combine Chinese salt, sugar, mustard, soy sauce, wine, lemon juice, boiled oil, sesame oil and pepper to form salad dressing. Add dressing to chicken; mix well. Add coriander, green onions and sesame seeds. In large bowl place lettuce; add chicken mixture and toss. Lettuce may also be used as bedding on serving platter, instead of combining it. At last minute lightly toss in bean threads, mixing until moistened by dressing. Serve in bowl or on platter. Garnish with thin, 2-inch strips of ham or prosciutto, if desired. Makes 3 to 4 servings.

CHICKEN BREASTS EN GELEE

Luscious black grapes and a light jelly glaze touched with Madeira top these poached chicken breasts. Low in calories, high in flavor and beauty.

4 *whole chicken breasts,*
  halved
Salt
1½ *cups chicken broth*
1 *carrot, peeled, sliced*
1 *slice onion*
2 *whole cloves*
1 *sprig parsley*

½ *teaspoon tarragon leaves*
1 *envelope unflavored gelatine*
¼ *cup Madeira wine*
Lemon juice
1 *cup black grapes*
Long strips lemon peel, bits
  orange peel, chicory or
  watercress

Sprinkle chicken very lightly with salt, place skin-side up in saucepan. Add broth, carrot, onion, cloves, parsley and tarragon. Cover and simmer gently until tender, about 30 minutes. Cool slightly in broth and pull off skin. (Lift meat off bones, if you wish.) Wrap chicken in saran film and chill. Chill broth enough to skim off fat layer; strain. There should be 1½ cups. Add water if necessary. Sprinkle gelatine over broth in saucepan; stir over low heat until it is melted, 2 or 3 minutes. Add Madeira, a few drops lemon juice and salt if needed. Chill until syrupy. Brush lightly over chicken breasts. Halve and seed a few of the grapes; press cut-side down on chicken in a pretty flower design using long, thin strips of lemon peel for stems and orange for centers of flowers. Glaze with second coat of thick-but-not-set aspic. This requires about ½ to 1 cup aspic. Chill rest of aspic firm in shallow pan; cut into tiny cubes and pile around chicken on platter if desired. Decorate with rest of grapes and chicory or watercress. Makes 4 servings.

BREASTS OF CHICKEN JEANNETTE

Of all the cold chicken dishes this is one of the most famous. It was introduced by Escoffier for his elegant cold tables at the impeccable old Hotel Savoy in London. You can duplicate it for a spectacular luncheon party dish or buffet by following these three, not-too-difficult steps. First poach and cool chicken breasts; next make the satiny white jellied sauce to mantle the chicken. Finally, decorate it and glaze with a shiny clear aspic.

2 large whole chicken breasts
  (fryers or roasters)
Piece cut lemon
2 cups chicken broth
1 slice onion
½ teaspoon salt, or to taste
Herb bouquet of 2 sprigs
  parsley, 1 teaspoon dried
  tarragon leaves,
  4 peppercorns, 1 whole
  clove

¼ cup pâté de foie gras or
  other light liver pâté
Chaud Froid Sauce*
Blanched tarragon or
  watercress leaves
Cutouts of truffles or ripe
  olives
3 cups Crystal Aspic* made
  with chicken stock

Rub chicken with cut lemon and place in large saucepan with chicken broth, onion, salt and herb bouquet tied loosely in cheesecloth. Cover and cook gently with barely a bubble breaking the surface, until tender, about 30 minutes.

Remove chicken to cool. Strain and cool broth for chaud froid sauce. Cover cooled chicken with saran film and refrigerate. Make chaud froid sauce as directed. Pull skin off chicken. Slip point of knife between meat and bone and lift meat off each breast in two fillets. Slice each fillet in two lengthwise and arrange in a neat, symmetrical pattern on serving platter. Trim off any taggy edges and flatten each slice slightly to make an even flat surface. Spread each with a thin layer of pâté, then mantle with thickened chaud froid sauce. Chill until sauce sets, then cover evenly with rest of chaud froid. Chill until set, about 1 hour. Decorate chicken in a rather formal design with tarragon or watercress leaves and diamond cutouts of truffles or ripe olives, dipping them in syrupy thick aspic first. Spoon a light film of aspic over each slice and chill until set.

Pour remaining aspic into shallow pan and chill until set. To serve, trim any dribbles of chaud froid sauce from around chicken so shapes are well defined and wipe platter clean. Chop rest of aspic and place in heaps around chicken. Makes 8 servings.

CHAUD FROID SAUCE

A delicate Velouté or stock-based white sauce that gels with a glossy shine when cooled. Made with various stocks it's often used to coat a number of cold dishes—fish, turkey, a whole chicken. See our unusual variation in Ham with Chaud Froid Glaze.*

1 envelope unflavored gelatine
2 cups cooking broth from
   chicken above
2 tablespoons butter or
   margarine

2 tablespoons flour
2 egg yolks
½ cup cream
Salt, white pepper, nutmeg

Soften gelatin in ½ cup of the cold cooking broth. Melt butter in small heavy saucepan and stir in flour. Cook and stir over low heat without browning about 2 minutes. With small wire whisk stir in remaining cooking broth and cook a few minutes. Whisk in softened gelatine; cook and stir until sauce thickens (it will be a light, thin sauce). Beat egg yolks lightly with cream; stir in a little of the hot white sauce, then stir all back into sauce. Cook one-half minute longer. Season well with salt, pepper and a generous pinch of nutmeg. Cool in refrigerator or pan of ice, stirring often, until it begins to gel. Makes about 2½ cups.

JELLIED CHICKEN TARRAGON

An old-fashioned summer favorite with new ease, new flavor.

3½ cups chicken broth
2 teaspoons dried tarragon
   leaves
1 slice each onion and lemon
3 large, whole chicken breasts,
   split
Salt and white pepper

3 tablespoons minced parsley
1 cup cooked peas
2 envelopes unflavored gelatine
½ cup Madeira
Salad greens
Lemon Mayonnaise*

In large saucepan, heat broth, tarragon, onion and lemon to boiling. Lower to simmering. Season chicken with salt and white pepper; place in broth. Cover and simmer gently until tender, about 30 minutes. Quick-chill in refrigerator so fat layer will rise to top; skim it off. Skin and bone chicken; cut or slice into generous chunks. Mix gently with parsley and peas. Arrange in 6-cup mold rinsed in cold water. Strain broth and heat. Sprinkle gelatine over wine and dissolve in broth. Pour over chicken. Cover and chill until firm, 4 hours or more. Unmold on crisp greens. Slice and serve with lemon mayonnaise. Makes 8 servings.

Lemon Mayonnaise—Stir 2 tablespoons lemon juice, 2 teaspoons grated lemon peel into 1 cup mayonnaise.

TURKEY ROLL, CONTEMPO

Frozen boneless turkey roasts are easy to carve and serve for buffets and large parties and popular with the busy hostess. Our way of cooking them departs from the orthodox roasting method. Instead, we braised them in dry white wine and chicken broth, which gives delicious moist white meat, tender and tasty when chilled and sliced. Several other sauces are suggested besides the delicious homemade chutney.

Most of the roasts are wrapped in foil and packed in a foil baking pan. Loosen foil wrap and pour ½ to 1 cup dry white wine or chicken broth or a mixture of the two around the roast. Roasts vary in size so use the lesser amount for the small roasts. Sprinkle meat with crumbled dried marjoram leaves and white pepper. Cover loosely with foil again leaving plenty of headroom. Braise in 400 degree F. oven 2 to 3½ hours, or until meat is tender, depending on size of roast. If you have a meat thermometer, insert it after 1½ hours; roast until it registers 180 degrees F. Baste roast often with pan liquids. Open foil last half hour if you wish to brown roast lightly. Cool uncovered, then cover and chill. Slice and serve with Cranberry Chutney* or Ginger Mint Relish.*

TURKEY ROLL CHAUD FROID

Place cooked, chilled, trimmed turkey roll on serving platter. Mantle completely, in two applications, with chaud froid glaze used in Ham with Chaud Froid Glaze.* Sprinkle top, confetti-style, with finely diced bits of pimiento and green pepper.

STUFFED ROCK CORNISH HENS

Stuffed with pâté and glazed, these are elegant and delicious.

6 frozen Rock Cornish hens (about 1 pound each), defrosted
Salt and freshly ground pepper

Chicken Liver Pâté Stuffing*
½ cup butter or margarine
½ cup port wine
2 tablespoons bottled steak sauce

Defrost birds overnight in refrigerator. Remove giblets; save livers for pâté, use rest for stock or soup. Dry birds inside and out and rub inside with salt and pepper. Stuff with cool pâté; fasten opening with toothpicks. Put in shallow roasting pan. Melt butter, add wine and pour half of it over birds. Cover loosely with tent of foil. Roast at 400 degree F. 30 minutes, basting twice with the butter sauce. Remove foil. Add steak sauce to butter mixture; pour over birds. Roast, basting several times, until tender and glazed, 30 to 45 minutes longer. Cool and baste occasionally with pan glaze, if convenient. Wrap in saran film and refrigerate. Our favorite way is to remove pâté before serving birds. Serve it as first course with French bread. Serve birds with asparagus and a rice salad. Makes 6 servings (or 12 of ½ bird each).

Chicken Liver Pâté Stuffing

6 green onions
½ cup butter or margarine
1 pound chicken livers plus
    game hen livers
2 tablespoons cognac or
    brandy
½ pound coarsely chopped
    fresh mushrooms
1 teaspoon salt
Freshly ground black pepper
Generous pinch each nutmeg
    and thyme

½ cup port wine
1 slice French bread, coarsely
    crumbled
¼ clove garlic
2 sprigs parsley
2 teaspoons grated lemon peel
2 teaspoons lemon juice
2 eggs
¼ cup pistachio nuts, halved

Chop 4 onions and cook in half the butter 1 to 2 minutes. Blot chicken livers and livers from game hens dry on paper towels; add to onions. Cook and stir until lightly browned. Sprinkle with cognac; flame if you wish, then cook for 1 to 2 minutes. Add rest of butter, and heat; add mushrooms. Season with salt, pepper, nutmeg and thyme. Cook and stir about 3 minutes. Add wine and continue to cook a few minutes, until wine has evaporated slightly. Remove from heat; add the 2 onions, cut in pieces, and rest of ingredients except nuts. Whizz in blender (in two batches) turning motor on and off until mixture is minced, but not completely puréed. (Or mince or grind mixture and bind with eggs.) Add nuts. Cool. Stuff birds lightly using about ½ cup pâté for each. Makes about 3 cups.

CHICKEN LIVER APPETIZER

To serve pâté stuffing as an appetizer, follow recipe above except: Omit game hen livers. Cook all 6 green onions with the butter. Omit bread and eggs. Whizz all ingredients except pistachios in blender as described above. Add pistachios and pour into small crock or dish (about 2½-cup size). Cool and cover with a little melted butter. Cover and refrigerate overnight. Serve in crock or turn out on plate. Good with French bread, melba toast or crackers. Makes about 2½ cups.

JEWELED DUCK ASPIC

A Texas way to serve duck, completely devoid of the usual fattiness. It is conveniently boned and sliced, surrounded with a jewel-like setting of vegetables, then suspended in a zingy aspic.

4- to 5-pound duckling
1 large onion, quartered
2 stalks celery, cut up
2 whole carrots
1 cup vinegar
1 teaspoon salt
½ teaspoon pepper, or to taste

1 large tomato, peeled
Watercress
1 (or more) tablespoons beef or chicken extract
1 envelope unflavored gelatine

Thaw frozen duckling ahead of time. Remove skin, inserting point of small sharp knife between skin and flesh. With help of fingers pull and strip off skin. Cut duck into halves or quarters, and fit into soup pot with onion, celery, carrots, vinegar, salt and pepper. Add just enough water to cover. Bring to boil, skim and simmer until liquid is reduced to one-half and duck is tender, about 1½ hours. Remove duck and reserve carrots. Discard onion and celery. Strain broth through layers of cheesecloth and reserve; it should measure about 2 cups, but it does not need to be accurate. When meat is cool, bone it and cut into pieces about 1½ to 2 inches long. Slice tomato and arrange in aspic mold or large shallow glass casserole dish (8×12×2 inches). Arrange pieces of duckling and sliced carrots in mold attractively. Add small sprigs of watercress to arrangement. Bring about 2 cups broth to boil. Add extract to taste. Correct for tartness and add more vinegar, if needed. Check for salt and pepper. Sprinkle gelatine on ¼ cup cold water, add to hot broth and stir to dissolve. Pour over duck and vegetables; cool. Chill 4 hours or more. To complement this duck aspic, serve hot French bread spread with herb butter, a salad and your favorite wine. Makes 4 to 6 servings.

Note: If desired, cut duck skin in strips or squares, heat in skillet and render until crisp. Salt when done. Serve with crackers for cocktail appetizers.

JELLIED ORANGE DUCKLING

Friends in France often urge us to try turnips, olives, cherries and such with duckling. We do, then go right back to one of the best, most natural combinations of all—duckling with orange. Here it's braised, rather than roasted, to give juicier meat, a more flavorful aspic.

4- to 5-pound duckling	1½ tablespoons lemon juice
1 teaspoon salt	2½ cups clear chicken stock
Freshly ground pepper	(or strained stock made
¼ teaspoon dried thyme	from duck neck, giblets,
leaves, crumbled	wing tips and seasoning
3 large navel oranges	herbs)
1 tablespoon butter	1½ envelopes (1½
1 onion, chopped	tablespoons) unflavored
1 carrot, chopped	gelatine
¾ cup port or Madeira	Watercress or parsley
2½ tablespoons sugar	

Wash duckling; dry with paper towels and prick all over with fork. Pull out all excess fat and season inside with salt, pepper and thyme. Fasten openings with skewers and tie duckling in neat, compact shape. Rub over skin with half of one orange. In heavy pan or Dutch oven, brown lightly in butter (this is only to develop flavor in braising liquid since skin will be discarded). Add onion, carrot, the orange half cut in pieces and ½ cup wine. Cover and braise in 350 degree F. oven about 2 hours, or until meat is tender. Spoon or siphon off fat with bulb baster as it accumulates and baste duck occasionally with pan juices.

In small heavy pan, combine sugar and lemon juice; stir over medium heat till mixture bubbles and turns a golden caramel color. Off heat add ½ cup of the stock and remaining wine. Stir over high heat to melt caramel syrup; boil a few minutes to reduce to about ½ cup. Remove yellow peel from rest of oranges with vegetable peeler and cut into thin, pin-size slivers. Simmer in about 3 cups water 10 minutes. Drain and blot dry. Remove cooked duckling from pan; cool and chill. Drain off pan juices; let settle a few minutes and

Plate No. 2-A mouth-watering mosaic of colorful vegetables, seafood and cheese called *Greek Salata* (p. 104). Photograph courtesy of Hellmann's/Best Foods Mayonnaise.

skim off fat. Reduce to ¼ cup by boiling a few minutes. Strain through several layers wet cheesecloth. In saucepan, sprinkle gelatine over remaining cold stock (clarified stock is nice but not absolutely necessary). Stir over low heat until gelatine melts. Add caramel mixture, the pan liquid and orange peel. Taste and add more wine, lemon juice or salt if needed to give aspic a definite sweet-sour tang. Chill until syrupy thick.

Peel oranges and slice into cartwheels; cut in half. Skin duckling and carve breast and legs into neat slices for top of dish. Remove rest of meat from bones in strips and pieces. Place layer of duckling in deepish platter or dish; arrange oranges slices on each side; cover with layer of aspic. Cover with slightly overlapping duckling slices. Add more orange slices to make an attractive arrangement; cover completely with aspic. Chill several hours, until set. Decorate end of platter with a bouquet of watercress or parsley. Makes 4 to 6 servings.

Complement this flavorful dish with a clear hot soup, a light rice or French Potato Salad* and creamy Mousse au Chocolat.*

PEPPER ROAST

Though an inexpensive roast this is the secret of its tender rosy slices—it must be cooked rare, chilled well and sliced very, very thin.

4- to 5-pound boneless, rolled
  beef roast[2] (sirloin tip,
  English-cut, cross-rib, etc.[3])
Cut clove garlic
Olive oil
Salt

1 tablespoon crushed rosemary
  leaves
1 to 2 tablespoons coarsely
  crushed whole peppercorns
Sharp knife for carving

Rub meat with garlic, a little oil, plenty of salt and the rosemary. Place peppercorns between sheets of foil and crush coarsely with

[2] *Tenderizer:* Sprinkle meat with an unseasoned meat tenderizer as directed on label, if you wish. Or marinate several hours in 2 cups dry red wine, turning often, before you season meat. Dry with paper towels. Roast may be cooked on rotisseire, if preferred.

[3] *Ribs of Beef:* Boned and rolled ribs of beef may be given the pepper treatment as above, but we prefer it seasoned more simply, and cooked with the bone in. For cold platters and buffets, it may be thickly sliced, but several elegantly thin slices are easier to manage.

side of kitchen mallet or hammer. Press into beef all over with heel of your palm. Cover loosely with foil or saran film; let stand a couple of hours. Place in shallow pan and, if you have it, insert meat thermometer through thickest part to halfway point. Roast at 350 degrees F. until thermometer registers 130 degrees F. (The lowest marking is 140 degrees F., so lift it out of meat after 1½ hours to check. Reinsert and check again when you think it's reached the estimated 130 degrees F. The thermometer climbs past 145 degrees F. within 15 minutes after roast is removed from oven, which means the meat is still cooking inside. If you have no meat thermometer, allow 2 to 2¼ hours for this size roast. Time depends on thickness as much as weight, but the less tender cuts must be cooked rare or medium-rare to taste tender when sliced. Cool roast; cover with saran film and chill. Slice very, very thin with sharp knife. Serve with mustards, fiery or mild, French and rye breads, pickles and cherry tomatoes and potato salad. Makes 8 to 10 servings.

BEEF AND MUSHROOMS VINAIGRETTE

Any thinly sliced cold roast beef is delicious in this arrangement. A rib roast or roasted fillet is especially good.

1 large white Bermuda onion	*1 teaspoon brown prepared*
12 to 15 large fresh	*mustard*
mushrooms	*Pinch each dried marjoram*
Salt and lemon juice	*and chervil, crumbled*
1½ pounds cold beef roast,	*Freshly ground pepper*
thinly sliced	*½ cup salad oil*
¼ cup red wine vinegar	*2 tablespoons chopped parsley*

Peel onion, slice thinly and separate into rings. Rinse mushrooms and drop into boiling water adding a pinch of salt, a few drops of lemon juice. Remove mushrooms immediately; blot dry on paper towels and slice lengthwise rather thickly. Drop onion rings into the boiling water; remove immediately. Drain on paper towels. Arrange meat, onion and mushrooms attractively on serving platter in neat rows or groups. Blend vinegar into mustard, then stir in herbs, salt and pepper to taste. Gradually blend in oil. Pour over platter arrangement. Cover with saran film and chill several hours. Baste occasionally. Scatter parsley on top. Makes 4 to 6 servings.

COLONEL BEACH'S BEEF SUPREME

Though a typhoon wiped out Colonel Donn Beach's floating restaurant, the Hong Kong Lady, his marvelous recipe that originated there survived. The special flavor comes from a marinade of Roquefort cheese, coffee and vermouth.

½ cup olive oil
1 large clove garlic, crushed
1 teaspoon salt
½ teaspoon coarsely ground
   black pepper
½ teaspoon dry mustard
⅛ teaspoon monosodium
   glutamate

1½ tablespoons Roquefort
   cheese
2 teaspoons instant coffee
2 tablespoons dry vermouth
4 pounds choice New York
   strip or sirloin steak, 1¾
   inches thick, well trimmed

Blend olive oil and all other ingredients except steak together into a thick sauce. Rub well into steak and marinate at room temperature for at least 3 hours. Broil 10 minutes on one side, turn and broil 10 minutes on other. Repeat once more. Total cooking time is about 40 minutes for medium-rare. Turn meat with long-handled tongs—a fork would release meat juices. Brush on marinade frequently while steak is broiling. When done, cool; wrap in saran film or foil and refrigerate. To serve, slice across grain in very thin slices, at about a 30-degree angle. Makes 6 to 8 servings. With it you might serve a lightly dressed salad of watercress and pimientos, crisp potatoes or bread of your choice. For dessert, Donn suggests strong black coffee laced with a spoonful of orange honey and ½ ounce Jamaica rum.

BEEF DAUBE GLACE

This savory concoction of beef, marinated in wine and a rich assortment of herbs, then slowly braised, is named for its cooking pot or casserole called *daubière*. Each French province makes it differently —and deliciously. You can eliminate the larding, if you prefer, but it does add rich flavor well worth the effort. The several steps involved here require very little time, they're just spread out over 3 different days.

4 to 5 pounds boneless beef
  rump or round
4 slices lean bacon
2 cloves garlic
2 tablespoons minced parsley
½ teaspoon each thyme and
  marjoram
2 cups dry red wine
  (a California Cabernet
  Sauvignon, Bordeaux or
  light Burgundy)
2 onions, sliced
2 crumbled bay leaves

1 tablespoon salt
1 teaspoon coarsely cracked
  peppercorns
4 whole allspice
6 to 8 carrots, scraped and
  sliced
1 veal knuckle, cracked
1 pork shank, split or cracked
2 cups beef stock or canned
  bouillon
Garnishes of minced parsley,
  cherry tomatoes, cooked
  vegetables, and lettuce cups

You may just dump all the ingredients except garnishes together with the beef into a large non-metallic bowl to marinate for 24 hours. But here's how to lard the beef. Simmer bacon in water to cover 10 minutes; drain, rinse and dry. Crush 1 clove garlic and mix with parsley, thyme and marjoram. Spread on bacon and roll up from the long side into pencil-like strips. Make 4 incisions in beef with larding needle or long metal skewer; push bacon rolls into meat. Place meat in deep bowl. Add wine, onions, bay leaves, salt, pepper and allspice. Marinate 24 hours. You're free of this now till next day, except to turn it several times if you pass through the kitchen. Place meat with marinade, carrots, veal knuckle and pork shank, in large heavy casserole. Add bouillon and remaining garlic, chopped. Cover tightly and braise in very slow oven (250 degrees F.), until meat is fork-tender, 5 to 6 hours. (While this cooks, you're free again to run errands, clean the house, read a book.) Remove knuckle and shank. Strain broth through several layers of wet cheesecloth. Chill enough to skim off the fat layer. Chill. Chill meat enough to slice thinly. Fit slices neatly (like bread slices) into glass loaf pan or terrine. Heat broth and pour carefully over meat. Chill overnight. Turn out onto serving platter and top with minced parsley. Surround with cherry tomatoes and bouquets of cooked vegetables heaped in crisp lettuce cups. Tiny whole carrots and green beans, cooked lightly and marinated in Sauce Vinaigrette* are especially appropriate and pretty. Makes 6 to 8 servings.

COLD BEEF TONGUE

Oxtunga

The red of the meat and the green of the sauce sounds like a Christmas decoration, but it's a splendid combination of flavors all year round.

1 smoked beef tongue	2 bay leaves
1 large onion, sliced	½ teaspoon whole allspice
2 sprigs parsley	1 teaspoon peppercorns
1 stalk celery with leaves	Sauce Verte,* optional

Wash tongue thoroughly in warm water; place in Dutch oven and cover with water. Bring slowly to boiling point; boil 5 minutes and skim. Add onion, parsley, celery and seasonings; reduce heat and simmer covered 3 to 4 hours, until fork-tender. Place in cold water to help loosen the skin; remove skin and cut away the roots. Cool, then wrap and chill in refrigerator 4 hours or overnight. Serve cut in thin slices on a platter with sauce verte in a dish, if so desired. Makes 6 to 8 servings.

TONGUE MOUSSE INDIENNE

If you think you don't like tongue, try this spicy mold first. It will convince you to use it more often.

1 smoked beef tongue (3 to 4 pounds)
2½ cups consommé
2 envelopes unflavored gelatine
2 teaspoons curry powder
¼ cup grated onion

1 teaspoon prepared mustard
2 tablespoons lemon juice
½ cup mayonnaise
1 cup heavy cream, whipped
Chicory
Chutney Dressing*

Cook, skin and cool tongue by basic directions for Cold Beef Tongue.* Put through meat grinder twice using finest blade or whizz in blender with part of consommé. (You should have 3½ to 4 cups.) Sprinkle gelatine and curry powder over cold consommé in saucepan. Stir over low heat until gelatine is melted. Cool a few minutes and stir in tongue, onion, mustard and lemon juice. Chill until cold and heavy, but not set. Fold in mayonnaise, then whipped cream. Pour carefully into 6-cup mold dipped in cold water. Cover with saran film and chill until firm, 4 hours or more. Unmold onto serving platter and garnish with frills of chicory. Serve with chutney dressing. Makes 6 to 8 servings.

Variations: All or part of the tongue may be replaced by 3 to 4 cups ground cooked ham, chicken, turkey or veal or a mixture of these.

VITELLO TONNATO

The wildest combination . . . veal, tuna and anchovies . . . produces a most elusive flavor in this beautiful, classic Milanese dish. You'll never believe it until you try it.

3½ pounds boneless rolled leg of veal
1 large onion, cut in quarters
2 carrots, cut in 2-inch pieces
2 celery stalks with leaves, cut in 2-inch pieces
2 sprigs parsley
2 cloves garlic, crushed
1 can (6½ to 7 ounces) tuna
1 can (2 ounces) flat anchovy fillets with oil

2 cups dry white wine
2 bay leaves
1 teaspoon rosemary
5 peppercorns
1 cup mayonnaise
¼ cup lemon juice
Salt to taste
Sliced black olives, pimiento bits, lemon slices, watercress

Place meat in large heavy pot or Dutch oven. Add vegetables, parsley, garlic, tuna and anchovies with oil, wine, herbs and peppercorns. Cover pot securely and simmer approximately 2 hours, until meat is quite tender. Remove meat from pot and cool. Wrap in saran film and refrigerate 4 hours or overnight. Reduce sauce in pot by boiling gently uncovered until it is half as much. Force through a fine sieve or better, whizz in a blender until smooth. Chill. Before serving blend in mayonnaise and season to taste with lemon juice and salt. Slice veal thinly, on a slant. Arrange on serving dish, overlapping slices slightly. Mask with sauce. Garnish with sliced black olives and pimiento bits, lemon slices and sprigs of watercress. Nice with Risi Bisi Salad* and French bread. Makes 6 servings.

JELLIED PORK AND VEAL
Sylta

A family recipe, traditionally around at our Christmas smörgåsbords, that is both inexpensive and impressive. It's especially good with sassy pickled beets.

2-pound cut fresh pork shank
   or front hock
2-pound cut veal shank
2 quarts water
1½ tablespoons salt
½ teaspoon whole peppercorns
1 teaspoon whole allspice
6 whole cloves
2 bay leaves
1 large onion, peeled

1 carrot, peeled
2 sprigs parsley
1 envelope unflavored gelatine
2 tablespoons pickled beet
   juice
2 tablespoons white vinegar
¼ teaspoon ground white
   pepper
Vinegar Beets*
Parsley

In a large saucepan or Dutch oven, cover meat with water. Let boil and skim. Add seasonings, cloves, bay leaves, vegetables and parsley, excluding items listed after gelatine. Simmer covered 1½ to 2 hours, until meat is tender. Remove meat and cool. Trim meat from bones, discard fat and rind. Dice into ¼-inch cubes or run through coarse blade of meat grinder. Replace bones in stock. Reduce stock by simmering uncovered 40 minutes. Strain through several layers of wet cheesecloth. Replace meat in stock; reheat 10 minutes. Measure for 6 cups meat and broth. Sprinkle gelatine over beet juice (borrow some from vinegar beets, it's mainly for color), then stir into meat and broth. Add vinegar and pepper to taste. Lightly oil 1½-quart loaf pan or mold. Pour in gelatine-meat mixture, let cool. Cover and refrigerate. Check and skim any fat that rises later. Chill until well set, 4 hours or overnight. Unmold on cold serving dish. Garnish with vinegar beets and parsley sprigs. Slice to serve. Makes 10 servings.

COLD GLAZED HAM

Baked-in spices give this modern, fully cooked ham an old-fashioned flavor resembling that of country hams. Serve it cold, sliced elegantly thin. For a special buffet, the snowy Ham with Chaud Froid Glaze,* which follows, makes an outstanding display.

1 fully cooked, smoked ham
   (or half) 8 to 10 pounds
1 teaspoon black pepper
1 tablespoon ground cloves

2 tablespoons dry mustard
1 cup Madeira or cream sherry
½ cup orange or ginger
   marmalade

Trim most of fat from ham and place in roasting pan. Make a paste with pepper, cloves, mustard and a couple spoonfuls of wine; pat onto ham. Pour wine into pan; cover loosely with tent of foil. Bake at 325 degrees F. about 15 minutes per pound, or by wrapper directions. After 1 hour, remove foil; baste ham often with wine. Pour off drippings and skim off fat. If any fat remains on ham, score in traditional diamond pattern if desired. Blend 1 to 2 tablespoons fat-free drippings with marmalade; spread over ham. Cook until lightly glazed, about 30 minutes. Cool ham; refrigerate in saran film. Serve in thin slices. Makes 12 or more servings.

HAM WITH CHAUD FROID GLAZE

The shiny white glaze starts with an aspic base rather than the cream sauce or Velouté of traditional chaud froid sauce. It's a variation of one we learned from Madame Simone Beck of Paris—author, teacher and culinary expert extraordinaire.

Cold baked ham
2 envelopes unflavored gelatine
2½ cups cold, fat-free chicken
   broth
3 tablespoons Madeira or
   cream sherry
1 teaspoon dry mustard
1 cup dairy sour cream
1 cup heavy cream

Salt and monosodium
   glutamate
Sliced carrot cutouts, green
   pepper slivers, drained
   pineapple tidbits, blanched
   parsley leaves, blotted dry,
   for decorations
About 1 cup Crystal Aspic*

Bake ham by directions for Cold Glazed Ham.* Cut off fat and skin. Omit marmalade glaze. Chill ham in saran film. In saucepan, sprinkle gelatine over cold broth. Stir over low heat until clear and gelatine melts. Blend wine into mustard; stir into broth. Cool slightly and gradually stir in sour cream, then heavy cream. Season with dash of salt and monosodium glutamate. Chill until thick but not set, stirring often. Set ham on wire rack over sheet of foil. Spoon part of glaze over all in thin even layer. Chill until set, just a few minutes. Spread with second layer of glaze coating ham completely in a snowy mantle. Dribbles that fall can be reused. As you work, keep glaze thick, but spoonable, by setting bowl either in pan of ice cubes or warm water, as necessary. Decorate glaze with flower design or whatever suits the occasion with materials suggested. Dip each in a little syrupy crystal aspic and affix to glaze. Chill. Makes about 4½ cups chaud froid glaze, enough for a 10 to 12 pound ham.

JAMBON PERSILLE

Ham in Parsley Aspic

A Burgundian specialty of ham and parsley in a wine-flavored aspic. It resembles a dish we've enjoyed at the Hotel de la Poste in Beaune, France, center of the famous Burgundy wine country.

2 cups dry white Burgundy
  or other white wine
2 cups chicken broth
6 whole black peppercorns,
  lightly crushed
1 onion, stuck with 2 cloves
½ carrot, sliced
½ lemon, sliced
1 bay leaf
¼ teaspoon thyme leaves
1 teaspoon dried tarragon
  leaves

Salt to taste (depends on
  type of ham)
5- to 6-pound piece, bone-in
  smoked ham
2 envelopes unflavored gelatine
2 egg whites and 2 egg shells
1 cup finely chopped parsley
Watercress or parsley
Mustard Fruit Mayonnaise*

Simmer together about 30 minutes the wine, broth, pepper, vegetables, lemon, herbs, salt and 2 cups water. Add ham and simmer until tender, 1½ to 2 hours. (If pre-cooked ham is used, simmer just long enough to heat ham through and allow it to absorb some of the flavors.) Cool ham in stock. Remove ham; strain stock and skim off fat. There should be about 3½ cups stock. Trim fat from ham and cut ham in small neat cubes or julienne strips (you should have about 5 cups). Place in 2-quart mold or terrine. In saucepan, combine stock, gelatine, lightly beaten egg whites and crushed shells. Follow directions for Clarified Stock.* If necessary, add water or white wine to make 3½ cups. Cool. Add parsley to mold; pour in gelatine to cover. Cover with saran film, chill overnight, or until set. Unmold ham on serving plate, and garnish with watercress or parsley. Serve with mustard fruit mayonnaise. Makes 8 to 10 servings.

MUSTARD FRUIT MAYONNAISE

Mix 1 cup mayonnaise with 1 tablespoon prepared Dijon mustard and ¼ cup chopped, mixed candied fruit. Makes about 1 cup.

CANTONESE ROAST PORK

Chinese Cha Siu

Roasting meat suspended in the oven is the neat trick of this famous dish—it's simply a matter of drapery hooks or safety pins!

2 pounds pork tenderloin
or very lean pork ribs
1 to 2 cloves garlic, crushed,
or to taste
1 teaspoon grated or crushed
fresh ginger root†[4]
2 scallions, minced
¼ cup soy sauce

¼ cup Hoisin sauce†[5]
¼ cup dry sherry
3 tablespoons catsup
1 tablespoon Chinese (hot)
chili sauce†[6]
Pinch Chinese 5-Spices†[7]
½ teaspoon salt
¼ cup honey

[4] If ginger root is unavailable, omit entirely in this recipe. A substitute may be rinsed preserved ginger.
[5] If Hoisin sauce is unavailable, the oriental seasoning may be somewhat missing but two tablespoons light or dark corn syrup may be substituted for consistency and sweetness in this recipe.
[6] If Chinese chili sauce is unavailable, Mexican hot sauce (Salsa Jalapeña) or Louisiana hot sauce may be substituted.
[7] If Chinese 5-Spices is unavailable, substitute allspice, cinnamon, cloves, ginger and nutmeg in very small quantities.

Use only very lean baby-type ribs or tenderloin, with no fat. Cut meat into 5- to 6-inch strips. Combine all ingredients except honey. Marinate meat in mixture 1 hour; baste and turn. Marinate 1 hour longer. Place one shelf at uppermost level and one at bottom of oven. Put drip pan partially filled with water on bottom rack to moisten oven air while roasting. Attach drapery hooks or large safety pins to one end of each meat strip. Brush honey on all sides of meat (it does not glaze in true Chinese style unless done by hanging method). Suspend each strip from a rung of upper rack, well over drip pan area. Cook at 275 degrees F. 30 minutes, 300 degrees F. 30 minutes, then at 400 degrees F. for 10 minutes. Cool, cover with saran film and refrigerate. To serve, cut tenderloin in thin diagonal slices and overlap pieces on platter. Cut spareribs into a rib or two, finger-food size, and heap on serving platter or bowl. No additional sauces are needed with this flavorful pork. Makes 4 to 6 servings.

PRESSED LAMB ROLL

Får Rulle

We found a butterflied leg of lamb or boned shoulder makes a leaner, tastier roll than the flank meat or breast suggested in original Norwegian pressed lamb recipes. Our American adaptation has the typical, unforgettable clove-y seasoning.

¾ pound lean veal, coarsely ground
¾ pound lean pork, coarsely ground
1 tablespoon salt, divided
¼ teaspoon allspice
¼ teaspoon ginger
½ teaspoon ground cloves

¼ teaspoon rubbed sage
¼ teaspoon thyme leaves
½ teaspoon coarsely ground black pepper
1 (5 to 6 pounds) leg of lamb, boned and butterflied (or a lean shoulder, boned for rolling)

Combine veal and pork with salt, allspice, ginger, cloves, sage, thyme and pepper using 1½ teaspoons salt. Have butcher bone lamb and butterfly (split almost through and lay open like a book, or butterfly) and pound slightly to flatten. Then spread with your mixture; roll and tie securely, cover with saran film and refrigerate overnight. Place roll in deep pot or Dutch oven; add water to half cover meat, sprinkle with remaining salt. Simmer, covered, about 2 hours, until tender. Remove meat from broth, cover loosely until cool and place a weight on top. Refrigerate overnight. Serve in thin slices. Good as smörgåsbord dish; goes well with Vinegar Beets* and French Potato Salad.* Makes 10 or more servings.

LAMB IN MINTY MARINADE

A blender-made sauce of vinaigrette, fresh mint and sour cream does wonderful things to cold cuts of roast lamb.

Seasoning salt
1 (5 pounds) leg of lamb
Bacon strips, optional
2 tablespoons lemon juice
6 tablespoons salad oil
⅛ teaspoon salt
Dash pepper
1 teaspoon rosemary
½ cup chopped fresh mint
  leaves

⅔ cup sour cream
Lettuce
1 large red onion, thinly
  sliced
1 green pepper, cut in strips
Pimiento strips
Lemon wedges
Fresh mint sprigs

Sprinkle seasoning salt over leg of lamb. Sear it uncovered for 15 minutes in 450 degree F. preheated oven, then cook at 350 degrees F. for 15 to 30 minutes to the pound (150 to 175 degrees F. on meat thermometer) according to your preference of doneness. If you wish to drape strips of bacon over the top of roast, this helps to self-baste it. When done let roast cool; then chill in refrigerator. After about 2 hours it can be thinly sliced, and much easier than when hot. Place sliced meat in rectangular baking pan; prepare marinade. Put lemon juice, salad oil, seasonings and herbs in blender. Whizz it. When herbs are almost puréed add sour cream. Whizz again, to blend. Pour sauce over meat coating all pieces. Cover pan and chill 2 hours or more. Arrange lettuce leaves on platter, place lamb with sauce on lettuce bed. Distribute sliced onion rings and green pepper strips over meat; add pimiento. Place lemon and fresh mint around rim of platter. Serve with Caponata.* Makes 6 to 8 servings.

CHINESE JELLIED LAMB
Young Kao

Lamb is typical of North China's meats, and surprisingly enough this jellied loaf is typical of ancient *winter* fare there. It has the color of natural, good brown stock with a meaty flavor.

2 to 3 pounds lamb stew
  meat (shoulder chops or
  stew cuts)
2½ cups water or stock
½ cup soy sauce
2 tablespoons dry sherry
2½ tablespoons sugar

2 carrots, cut in pieces
2 tablespoons unflavored
  gelatine
1 cup cold water
½ teaspoon salt
Chives

Put lamb into Dutch oven or heavy pot with snug cover. Combine next 4 ingredients, pour over meat. Add carrots. Cover pot and simmer about 2 hours, until lamb is quite tender. Remove from heat. Take meat from pot; remove fat and bones and dice meat. (It shreds as it is cut, which is fine.) Drain liquid in pot; reserve 2 cups. (Add water if liquid doesn't measure up.) Discard carrots. Return lamb meat to pot with 2 cups stock. Sprinkle gelatine over 1 cup cold water. Heat pot with meat and stock to boiling, add salt and stir while adding softened gelatine to it. When gelatine is dissolved, remove from heat and cool. Lightly oil a 1½-quart loaf pan; pour lamb and jelly into it. Chill in refrigerator, covered with saran film for 4 hours or overnight. Stir through it occasionally until it has set. To serve, unmold and cut loaf into cubes for an appetizer at the table or slice as a main course dish. Garnish with finely chopped chives. Makes 6 servings.

JELLIED EGG RING WITH DILLY TUNA

A doozy of a dish . . . easy and different . . . a most unusual molded egg salad paired with dill-flavored tuna.

2 envelopes unflavored gelatine
½ cup cold water
1 cup boiling water
¾ cup mayonnaise
1 teaspoon salt
1 clove garlic, crushed, optional
10 hard-cooked eggs

1 medium onion
1 green pepper
Lettuce or other greens
Dilly Tuna*
2 teaspoons minced pimiento
Fresh or dried dill
Tomatoes

Sprinkle gelatine over cold water. Dissolve in 1 cup boiling water. Cool. Blend in mayonnaise, salt and garlic. Cut cooled eggs, onion and pepper in chunks; run these through food grinder. Combine with gelatine mixture. Lightly oil 1½-quart ring mold and pour in mixture. Chill 4 hours or until set. Unmold on bed of lettuce on chilled platter. Fill center with dilly tuna, patted into dome shape with back of spoon. Sprinkle bits of minced pimiento over tuna. Garnish with dill and tomato wedges. Makes 8 to 10 servings.

Dilly Tuna

2 cans (6½ to 7 ounces each)
    tuna, with oil
¼ cup lemon juice
1 tablespoon minced fresh
    dill or 1½ teaspoons dried

2 teaspoons grated onion
Salt to taste
⅛ teaspoon hot pepper
    sauce,† optional

Drain oil from tuna in bowl. Add remaining ingredients, except tuna. Beat with fork. Add tuna and mix lightly. Cover and refrigerate 4 hours.

EGG MOLD INDIA

A crown of hard-cooked eggs in a golden curry aspic tops this creamy egg mold. A beautiful dish with lively flavor.

2 envelopes unflavored gelatine
2½ cups cold chicken broth
1 teaspoon curry powder
1 teaspoon salt
¼ cup vinegar
8 hard-cooked eggs
¼ cup chopped green onion
½ cup chopped green pepper
¼ cup chopped radishes
1 cup mayonnaise
Dash cayenne pepper
Small lettuce leaves
Cherry tomatoes

Sprinkle gelatine over 2 cups chicken broth in saucepan. Add curry powder and stir over low heat until gelatine is melted. Add salt and divide liquid in half. To one portion add remaining ½ cup broth and 3 tablespoons vinegar. Spoon a thin layer of this in bottom of 6-cup ring mold and chill until sticky-firm. Chill balance of this until syrupy thick. To remaining 1 cup gelatine add 1 tablespoon vinegar and cool slightly. Blend in 4 eggs finely chopped, the chopped vegetables and mayonnaise. Season with a dash of cayenne. Set aside or chill briefly. Cut rest of eggs in halves lengthwise and place cut-side down in jelly layer. Spoon in a little of the syrupy gelatine to set eggs in place. Chill a moment, then cover with rest of syrupy clear gelatine. Chill until sticky firm and spoon creamy mixture on top. Cover with saran film and chill until firm, 4 hours or more. Unmold on chilled plate and ring with small lettuce leaves. Decorate with bright cherry tomatoes. Makes 6 to 8 servings.

ALPINE CHEESE SOUFFLE

Here's a soufflé that won't unnerve a hostess. It's a fondue-flavored puff of fluff that stays picture-pretty, no matter when it's served.

3 envelopes unflavored gelatine
½ cup water
3 tablespoons butter
⅓ cup flour
1¾ cups milk
6 eggs, separated
1 cup grated Switzerland
  Swiss cheese
¾ teaspoon nutmeg
1 teaspoon salt
¼ teaspoon white ground
  pepper

¼ teaspoon monosodium
  glutamate
½ cup dry sherry
3 tablespoons kirsch
Few drops yellow food
  coloring, optional
1 cup heavy cream
Pimientos
Watercress

Tear a 2-foot strip of foil to make a collar around outside of 1-quart soufflé dish. Fold strip lengthwise in half, fit it snugly and lock ends, then tie it securely. Lightly oil inside of strip.

Sprinkle gelatine over water. In a saucepan melt butter, stir in flour and cook this roux over low heat stirring constantly. Add milk gradually; beat it in with wire whisk.

Cover pan and cook about 5 minutes over low heat until thickened and smooth. Blend some of cream sauce into beaten egg yolks. Pour back into saucepan. (Check for any lumps, if so strain mixture.) Cook a few minutes and stir constantly. Remove from heat; add softened gelatine and stir to dissolve it. While still hot add cheese, nutmeg and seasonings. Stir to help melt cheese. Add sherry and kirsch; add drops of food coloring, if desired. Cool it. Then chill until partially set. Whip cream stiff. Whip egg whites stiff, but not dry. Fold cream into cheese mixture, then fold in whites. Pour soufflé into dish. Chill 4 hours or more. After carefully removing foil collar, serve in soufflé dish. Garnish top with colorful strips of pimiento set out in an attractive design with scattered bits of watercress. Like cheese fondue, this soufflé is good partners with crusty French bread. A lightly seasoned tossed green salad makes a complete luncheon. Makes 6 to 8 servings.

CHAPTER V

Salads and Vegetables ⤲

Simple or spectacular, salads are superb! Light . . . filling, slimming . . . fattening, they fit everywhere, and into them almost anything goes. Salmagundi (that's potpourri in salad language) should be the byword. Here's where all that imagination and artistic expression you have can run barefoot. That is why our collection is varied . . . not vast. We want to steer you along the leafy green way, with some chilled recipes and a few pointers . . . the rest is a matter of taste, ours, yours and theirs.

First, don't let salads spook you! They can be fresh and crisp, chilling while waiting. They can be professional-looking unblemished molds extracted without fear (see Know-how chapter—To Unmold an Aspic). They can be marinated marvels, prepared long ahead. It's possible.

Salad success depends on "look-appeal," then taste. "Rabbit food" eaters take note; the simplest tossed green salad can lump into a fiasco if rules are ignored. So, DO . . . rinse leafy greens in lukewarm water, drain, tear them into bite-size pieces, wrap in a dry towel, then crisp and chill them in a refrigerator. "Head" lettuce comes clean and need not have a rinsing, unless you insist; so, pull off outer leaves, shred or cut lettuce and chill it.

Do . . . attend to your greens well ahead of time. Wet greens repel oil, oil repels vinegar, vinegar destroys connective tissue in greens and salt absorbs inner water content; result . . . a soggy mass!

Do . . . add those wet vegetables, like tomatoes, and damp fruits at the very last minute.

Do . . . dress your salad; don't *drown* it!

Do . . . toss it *gently*, if it's a tossed green salad you want and not a *black* and *blue* one!

Do . . . use an inspired hand with garnishing Be guided by our suggestions with the recipes, but don't be led. Try flowers, real and raw . . . edible nasturtium blossoms and leaves, "mums," borage, violets and rose petals . . . they are pretty and tasty in vegetable and fruit salads.

Do . . . invent absurd combinations, they could be clickers. Alfalfa sprouts in a tossed green salad stole the show at a recent buffet we had!

Salads are a merry métier . . . so, kick off your shoes and get to work. Here's to your own salmagundi!

LIMESTONE LETTUCE WITH EGG DRESSING

The sweet-sour taste of wilted lettuce salad with no droopy lettuce. A nice change.

2 heads limestone, butter or Bibb, lettuce
3 hard-cooked eggs
¼ cup sugar
½ teaspoon salt
½ teaspoon celery seed
⅓ cup salad oil
⅓ cup vinegar
Pepper, to taste

Rinse lettuce; wrap loosely in a clean towel and chill. Cook eggs. While eggs are warm, separate yolks and whites. Mash yolks and reserve whites. Combine sugar, salt, celery seed and oil with yolks; chill. Chop whites and chill. Just before serving break lettuce into bite-size pieces. Add vinegar to dressing mixture and shake. Toss chopped egg whites and salad dressing through lettuce. Add a grating of fresh pepper. Makes 6 servings.

SPINACH MUSHROOM SALAD

The crisp texture and delicate flavor of fresh raw mushrooms are a cool summery accent for spinach and romaine.

½ pound fresh young spinach leaves
½ head romaine
3 tablespoons white wine vinegar
2 teaspoons Dijon or other mild prepared mustard
1 teaspoon salt

Freshly ground black pepper
1 teaspoon sugar
1 tablespoon grated onion
½ cup salad oil
½ pound fresh mushrooms
4 radishes, thinly sliced
4 slices crisp-cooked bacon, crumbled

Trim and wash spinach thoroughly; blot dry with paper towels. Wash and dry romaine. Chill greens in clean towel or plastic bag. Combine next 7 ingredients in small jar and shake until well blended. Trim tip off mushroom stems. Wipe mushrooms with damp paper towels or rinse quickly and blot dry. Slice lengthwise. Break or cut greens into bite-size pieces into a large salad bowl (glass is pretty for this). Top with mushrooms and radishes and toss with just enough dressing to coat each leaf well. Add more salt and pepper if needed. Sprinkle with crumbled bacon. Serve on chilled plates. Makes 6 to 8 servings.

ANTIPASTO SALAD

A few Italian antipasto tidbits tossed with greens and zippy dressing make a hearty salad, ideal for a man's luncheon. Good too in smaller portions as a dinner first course.

½ head romaine
1 head butter lettuce or ½ head iceberg lettuce
½ cup thinly sliced radishes
½ cup sliced green onions
8 cherry tomatoes, halved or 1 large tomato, cut in wedges
1 can (3 ounces) tuna, drained
1 package (3 ounces) thinly sliced Genoa salami
1 package (6 ounces) mozzarella or provolone cheese, sliced

1 can (2 ounces) rolled anchovies with capers, drained
1 can (3⅞ ounces) pitted ripe olives
6 Italian pickled peppers (peperoncini)
Sauce Vinaigrette* or Anchovy Dressing*
Grated Romano or Parmesan cheese, optional

Rinse romaine and lettuce. Tear both into bite-size pieces. Wrap in a dry towel. Chill. Slice and keep separate, radishes, onions and tomatoes. Break tuna separately into small bits. Cut salami and cheese into ½-inch strips. Wrap in saran film and chill ingredients until needed. Serve in a large chilled bowl, arranging all tidbits in rows on top of salad greens. Garnish with anchovies, olives and peppers. Toss with a sauce vinaigrette or anchovy dressing; add a sprinkling of grated Romano or Parmesan cheese if desired. Makes 4 generous servings.

GREEK SALATA

From the Greek Sponge Colony in Tarpon Springs, Florida, comes this well-decorated, cone-shaped salad. Unlike other tossed green salads, this one is layered with flavors and surprises that tumble out with every serving.

1 pound (about 3) boiling potatoes in jackets
1 medium onion, finely chopped
3 tablespoons wine vinegar
1 teaspoon salt
½ cup mayonnaise
½ head lettuce, shredded
1 bunch romaine, large leaves only
12 watercress sprigs
3 stalks celery with leaves, finely chopped
½ green pepper, thinly sliced in rings
4 radishes, thinly sliced
4 green onions, thinly sliced
½ can (8¼ ounces) sliced beets
1 package (10 ounces) frozen cooked shrimp or ⅔ pound fresh, cooked shrimp

½ avocado, sliced in wedges
1 tablespoon lemon juice
1 medium cucumber, sliced
2 medium tomatoes, sliced lengthwise
4 Greek anchovies (others will do)
Sauce Vinaigrette*
½ teaspoon Worcestershire sauce
½ teaspoon sugar
½ teaspoon dried oregano leaves
8 Greek olives (ripe-type, others will do)
4 slices Greek feta cheese or Swiss cheese, cut in small slices

The night before, prepare potato part of salad. Boil potatoes in unsalted water, until almost tender. Do not overcook. When done, cool and peel. Slice potatoes, then halve slices. Add onion, sprinkle with vinegar and salt. Add mayonnaise; mix and chill. Discard outer leaves from lettuce; shred half of head, use remaining half elsewhere. Drain and towel dry romaine leaves and watercress. Wrap greens in towel and chill. The next day prepare celery, green pepper, radishes and onions; wrap individually and chill. Chill canned beets. Defrost shrimp, if frozen, and drain carefully. Close to serving time, slice

avocado and sprinkle with lemon juice. Prepare cucumbers and tomatoes. Rinse anchovies. Prepare sauce vinaigrette; add Worcestershire, sugar and oregano. Cover chilled platter with romaine leaves.
In the center place about 2 cups of potato salad shaped in a mound.
Cover this with shredded lettuce; sprinkle with some dressing. Now,
in layers, add the following, and sprinkle each with dressing: watercress, cucumber, celery, tomatoes, onions, green pepper and finally
avocado on top. Now, "hang ornaments" around the mound (like
a Christmas tree) in alternating circles, using radishes, beets, anchovies, olives, shrimp and cheese. Sprinkle outside of mound with more
dressing. Serve this salad-meal with slices of hot garlic toast. Makes
4 servings.

NASTURTIUM SALAD

Plant your own flower-salad garden tomorrow! You will like the
taste of nasturtiums . . . we did, after eating this salad at the Four
Seasons Restaurant in New York.

Pick and select a goodly group of tender, young nasturtium leaves
and a few blossoms. Rinse and wrap loosely in dry towel; chill.
Place leaves and blossoms in salad bowl and serve with Sauce
Vinaigrette,* ½ cup for 6 servings nasturtium greens.

EGGPLANT SALAD, MEDITERRANEAN

Serve this pickle-y eggplant as a relish or appetizer as is often done
in Mediterranean countries, or as we suggest, on cool sliced tomatoes
as a salad.

1 medium eggplant
Salt
1 clove garlic, chopped
4 tablespoons wine vinegar
½ teaspoon dried marjoram
    leaves, crumbled
¼ teaspoon dried crumbled
    sweet basil

2 tablespoons capers
Freshly ground black pepper
2 to 3 tablespoons olive oil
3 tomatoes, peeled and sliced
Parsley
Chicory or fresh fennel

Cut unpeeled eggplant in neat bite-size cubes and drop in boiling salted water. Simmer gently until crisp-tender and still shapely, 5 to 8 minutes. Drain and blot dry on paper towels. With wooden spoon crush garlic with ½ teaspoon salt in mixing bowl, then add vinegar, marjoram, basil, capers and a generous grinding of pepper. Add eggplant and mix gently; taste and add more salt if needed. Cover and chill. After eggplant has absorbed the vinegar mixture for an hour or so, toss gently with just enough olive oil to coat it lightly. Arrange tomatoes on platter or salad plates and top with mound of eggplant. Drizzle some of the marinade over tomatoes and sprinkle parsley over all. Decorate with tips of chicory or fennel. Makes 4 servings.

MUSHROOM SALAD FRANCAISE

Impressive as a first course or salad to accompany grilled chicken or steak or a poached fish.

1 pound fresh mushrooms
½ lemon
Sauce Vinaigrette* made with
  white wine tarragon vinegar
¼ cup minced parsley

2 tablespoons cut chives
Few leaves fresh tarragon,
  if available
Salt and white pepper
Boston lettuce

Rinse mushrooms quickly and drop into cool water to which juice of half a lemon has been added. Remove at once and blot dry. (Mushrooms soak up water like a sponge and will lose their delicate flavor and texture if allowed to soak.) Trim off tough tip of stems, then slice mushrooms lengthwise from stem into thick slices. Drop into bowl and sprinkle with a little vinaigrette as you work. When all are sliced, toss gently with parsley, chives and tarragon and just enough sauce to coat lightly. Add a little salt and pepper if needed. Cover with saran film and chill 1 hour. Heap in glass bowl rimmed with small leaves Boston lettuce or spoon into nest of lettuce on individual salad plates. Makes 6 servings.

Mushrooms-in-Cream Salad—Prepare mushrooms same as above. Toss with herbs and Lemon Cream Dressing.* Snips of fresh dill may replace tarragon.

TOMATOES CONTINENTAL

Instant salad platters, gala and refreshing. Each makes about 6 servings.

Tomatoes Napoli—Slice 6 large, firm-ripe tomatoes onto platter. Sprinkle with salt, freshly ground pepper and 4 chopped fresh basil leaves (or ½ teaspoon dried basil, crumbled). Put clove of garlic through press and add to ¼ cup olive oil. Drizzle half of it over tomatoes then sprinkle sparingly with 1 to 2 teaspoons wine vinegar. Rinse 6 large fresh mushrooms, dry on paper towels and slice lengthwise. Arrange over tomatoes. Season with salt, pepper, rest of oil and 2 to 3 teaspoons more vinegar. Cover with saran film and chill. Decorate platter with hot vinegar peppers and black olives.

Tomatoes Provençal—Slice 6 to 8 firm, medium-size tomatoes, in the French style, lengthwise from the stem. Place on platter. Scatter over them a cup or more tiny cooked shrimp. Add a large clove garlic, crushed, and ¼ cup capers to ½ cup Sauce Vinaigrette.* Blend well and pour over tomatoes. Serve at once, or chill and serve.

Tomatoes Remoulade—Slice 4 large tomatoes thickly and arrange on salad platter. Top each slice with hard-cooked egg halves. Mask eggs with Sauce Remoulade* (omit egg from sauce) and sprinkle parsley or capers on top.

Tomatoes Monterey—Slice 4 or 5 large firm-ripe tomatoes onto salad platter. Cover with 2 (4 ounces each) marinated artichoke hearts and their marinade. Cover with saran film and chill an hour or so. Remove from refrigerator 5 to 10 minutes before serving.

ARTICHOKE CAVIAR SALAD

Drain jar of 4 to 6 artichoke bottoms and marinate overnight in ½ cup Sauce Vinaigrette.* Blend ½ teaspoon grated onion and lime juice to taste in ½ cup dairy sour cream. Gently swirl into it a small jar of (about 2 tablespoons) black caviar. Set drained artichoke bottoms on nests of crisp shredded lettuce outlined with sprigs of watercress or parsley. Fill with sour cream mixture. Sprinkle chopped chives on top.

FRENCH POTATO SALAD

The French trick of pouring a little white wine or stock over warm potatoes before adding the dressing is a good one to know. Less oil is absorbed by potatoes, they are lighter, more flavorful.

2 pounds small boiling
  potatoes
Salt
2 tablespoons dry white wine
2 tablespoons light consommé
½ cup Sauce Vinaigrette*
2 teaspoons Dijon mustard

1 tablespoon chopped fresh
  tarragon and chervil, mixed
  (or 1 teaspoon dried mixed
  herbs)
2 tablespoons minced shallots
  or green onions
1 tablespoon minced parsley

Cook potatoes in boiling salted water until just tender. Drain, peel while warm and slice about ¼ inch thick. Mix wine and consommé and pour over them. Let stand until liquid is absorbed. Beat vinaigrette into mustard until smooth. Add herbs. Sprinkle shallots, parsley and dressing over potatoes. Toss gently until mixed. Taste and adjust seasonings. Cover and chill only until flavors blend. Serve cool, but not icy, in a pretty glass bowl. Sprinkle with more parsley if you wish. Makes 4 to 6 servings.

SALAD OLIVIER

This most famous of zakuska salads was created by M. Olivier, the French chef for Tsar Nicholas II. It was a simple French potato salad until he gave it a taste of Russian flavor and tsarist extravagance.

1 breast of chicken poached
  or boiled
3 (under 1 pound) medium,
  boiled, warm potatoes
2 tablespoons vinegar
½ teaspoon salt
Pepper to taste
2 small dill pickles

¼ cup mayonnaise
1 teaspoon Worcestershire
  sauce
1 or 2 hard-cooked eggs, cut
  in wedges
1 tomato, sliced in thin
  wedges
Sliced olives

Remove skin and fat from chicken. Cut meat into thin, even strips. While potatoes are warm, cut into ⅛ inch thick slices. Combine vinegar and salt and sprinkle over potatoes. Add pepper to taste and set aside. Peel pickles; slice thinly. Blend mayonnaise with Worcestershire. Combine chicken, pickle and potatoes. Add mayonnaise mixture; gently blend together. Place salad in bowl or flat zakuska-type dish (narrow, oval, inch-deep platter). Garnish with egg and tomato wedges, add circles of sliced olives. Duck may be substituted for chicken. It may be used as an hors d'oeuvres, a main course or buffet salad too. Depending on use it makes 4 to 8 servings.

SWISS AND POTATO SALAD

Two Swiss favorites—cheese and potatoes—combined in a hearty supper salad. Great for a buffet or outdoor party.

1 pound (4 or 5 small) boiling potatoes
Salt
6 tablespoons Sauce Vinaigrette* or bottled, light Italian-type dressing
½ pound aged Swiss Emmenthal cheese, diced (2 cups)
½ cup diced celery hearts

3 tablespoons minced green onions
3 tablespoons minced parsley
4 hard-cooked eggs
2 slices crisp-cooked bacon, crumbled
½ cup mayonnaise
½ teaspoon dry mustard
Wine vinegar, if needed
Freshly ground pepper

Cook potatoes in boiling salted water until just tender, but shapely. Peel while warm and sprinkle with ¼ cup vinaigrette or Italian dressing. Cool and combine with cheese, celery, onion, 2 tablespoons parsley, 3 eggs, chopped, and bacon. Mix mayonnaise with mustard and rest of vinaigrette. Thin with a little wine vinegar if necessary and pour over salad. Mix lightly, season with salt and pepper; chill. To serve, chop remaining egg fine and mix with remaining parsley; sprinkle over salad. Makes 6 servings.

DANISH MACARONI SALAD

Makaronisalat

Although we Americans may have thought this salad was our own idea . . . and a good one for picnics, at that . . . it is actually a classic on Danish Koldbord tables. Here's their way of doing it.

6 cups water
2 tablespoons salt
2 cups elbow macaroni
3 hard-cooked eggs
½ teaspoon dry mustard
1 teaspoon salt
⅓ cup mayonnaise
⅔ cup sour cream
2 tablespoons diced pimiento
1 cup minced Danish boiled
　ham or pork luncheon meat
Parsley or dill

Bring 6 cups water to boil with salt; add macaroni slowly and stir frequently. Cook about 10 to 12 minutes. Drain thoroughly and rinse with hot water. Cool. Mash yolks of 2 eggs; discard whites. Add mustard and salt to yolks. Blend in mayonnaise. Fold in sour cream. Add pimiento and ⅔ cup ham; combine with drained, cooled macaroni and chill. Garnish with remaining ham, egg cut in slices or wedges and minced fresh parsley or dill. Makes 8 or more servings.

SICILIAN BEAN SALAD

Look for an interesting variety of sausages to complete this robust salad. With soup, it's a meal.

1 can (20 ounces) garbanzo
　beans
1 can (20 ounces) red or
　white kidney beans
1 clove garlic
½ teaspoon salt
Pinch crushed, dried red
　pepper
½ teaspoon marjoram
⅓ cup red wine vinegar
4 to 6 anchovy fillets, drained
⅓ cup salad oil (part olive
　oil)
2 tablespoons minced parsley
1 sweet red onion, thinly
　sliced
Sausages (salami, cervelat,
　mortadella, galantina)
Crisp greens

Drain and rinse beans. Crush garlic in the salt with wooden spoon or mortar and pestle. Blend in red pepper, marjoram, vinegar and anchovies; then beat in oil. Pour over beans and refrigerate several hours. An hour before serving, mix in parsley and onion. Heap salad into bowl and arrange sausage around edge in neat overlapping slices or bundles of julienne strips. Use crisp snippets of escarole, chicory, fennel or Chinese celery-cabbage for greenery. Makes 6 servings.

RISI BISI SALAD

Rice Salad with Peas

1 cup long grain rice
1 teaspoon salt
Bay leaf
1 clove garlic
1 slice lemon
1½ cups cooked green peas
¼ cup chopped green onions
¼ cup diced green pepper
¼ cup diced, drained canned pimiento
2 tablespoons minced parsley
½ cup Sauce Vinaigrette*
Hearts chicory or escarole
½ cup pine nuts
3 hard-cooked eggs
3 small tomatoes

Cook rice by package directions adding salt, bay leaf, garlic and lemon to cooking water. (Or by our favorite way for flaky, dry rice—place rice in saucepan with 1¾ cups cold water and the seasonings. Cover tightly and heat to boiling. Turn heat to lowest; let rice steam 20 to 25 minutes, until all liquid is absorbed. Fluff with fork.) To hot rice add peas, green onions, green pepper, pimiento and parsley. Mix gently, with just enough vinaigrette to season well and coat rice—but be rather sparing. Pack into deepish bowl, cover and chill. Turn out on salad platter and circle with sprays of chicory or escarole. Sprinkle top with pine nuts. Stand thick slices egg and tomato wedges around base. Makes 4 to 5 servings.

WONDERFUL CHICKEN SALADS

Grandmother likely boiled a plump stewing hen for the sumptuous chicken salads that adorned her cold buffets and Sunday suppers. Ours are made with succulent poached chicken breasts, fast and easy. The variations are legion and nothing's more suitable or appealing for such occasions.

CHICKEN SALAD AMANDINE

4 whole chicken breasts,
  split and poached
2 cups thinly sliced celery
1 cup mayonnaise
½ cup heavy cream, whipped
Fresh lemon juice

Salt and cayenne pepper
Pinch each tarragon, chervil
  and nutmeg
Butter lettuce
1 cup (or more) whole
  blanched salted almonds

Poach chicken by directions for Breast of Chicken Jeannette.* Cool, remove skin and bones and cut chicken into ½-inch chunks. Mix with celery. Combine mayonnaise and cream and gently fold in. Season to taste with lemon juice, salt, cayenne, the herbs and nutmeg. Cover and chill. Mound on serving platter and ring with small lettuce leaves. Scatter almonds on top. Chopped toasted almonds may be mixed with salad and slivered almonds used as top garnish, but the whole salted almonds make an elegant, crisp contrast. Makes 8 or more servings.

Serve with hot biscuits or scones and Brandied Peaches.*

CHICKEN SALAD EXOTIQUE

2 small pineapples
4 cups cut-up poached
  chicken breasts (about 3
  whole breasts)
1 cup sliced water chestnuts
½ cup sliced celery

2 tablespoons chopped candied
  ginger
¾ cup mayonnaise
1 tablespoon chopped chutney
Lemon juice
Salt and nutmeg

Cut pineapples lengthwise in half through leafy crown. To remove meat, cut around pineapple ½ inch inside rind with long flexible knife. Cut down through meat in lengthwise and crosswise slices, keeping rind intact. With help of the flexible blade, scoop out meat leaving pineapple shell. Drain shells upside down on paper towels. Blot inside. Cut pineapple meat into chunks removing center core. Use about half of the meat for salad; store rest in covered dish for another meal. Mix chicken, water chestnuts, celery and ginger. Blend mayonnaise, chutney and lemon juice to taste. Pour over salad and mix gently. Season with salt and dash of nutmeg. Divide half the pineapple chunks among the pineapple shells; top with chicken salad. Decorate top with rest of pineapple. Cover with saran film and chill. Makes 4 big salads.

SALADE MIGNONNE

From New York's L'Etoile, a star-designed salad with an ethereal composition. It's julienned chicken and Belgian endive bound together in mayonnaise . . . simply elegant.

6 poached whole chicken breasts	Salt and pepper, to taste
1 pound Belgian endive	1 medium-size truffle,† finely chopped
1¼ cups mayonnaise	2 hard-cooked eggs, cut in quarters
1 cup heavy cream, whipped	

Cut chicken and three-fourths of endive into thin, matchlike strips. Blend mayonnaise lightly with whipped cream, salt and pepper; then mix in strips of chicken and endive. Place remaining endive leaves in a star form on bottom of salad bowl (or on individual salad plates). Put chicken mixture in center. Sprinkle with chopped truffle and garnish with egg wedges. Serve with crusty French bread. Makes 6 to 8 servings.

VEAL SALAD

Fleisch-salat

A favorite of many, this delicious German salad composed of veal, pickles and mayonnaise . . . it will be yours too.

2 cups (1 pound) cooked, cut-up veal
1¼ cups (½ pound) sliced boiled potatoes, optional
1 tart apple, cut up
2 sweet pickled gherkins, chopped
2 teaspoons capers

½ cup Sauce Vinaigrette*
1 teaspoon Dijon mustard
½ cup mayonnaise
Salt and pepper to taste
2 hard-cooked eggs, sliced
Chives or parsley
Lettuce
Vinegar Beets*

Dice or thinly slice veal in 1-inch strips. Slice or dice potatoes, if desired, and apple. Marinate veal, potatoes, apple, pickles and capers in vinaigrette (omit garlic) for 1 hour. Mix mustard with mayonnaise. Toss mayonnaise through salad; check seasoning. Add more mayonnaise, if desired. Place salad in serving bowl, cover with saran film and chill in refrigerator 4 hours or more. (It's often better the next day.) Garnish with sliced eggs and a sprinkling of chopped chives or parsley. Use lettuce leaves and vinegar beets for additional decoration. Makes 4 to 6 servings.

DILLED SHRIMP, AVOCADO

A quivery aspic of dill and shrimp heaped in luscious avocado halves. Serve as salad or soup.

1 envelope unflavored gelatine
2¼ cups clear, fat-free chicken broth
1 bay leaf, broken in pieces
½ teaspoon salt
1 teaspoon dried dill weed
2 tablespoons vinegar

1 tablespoon lemon juice
4 to 5 drops Tabasco
1 cup cooked, deveined shrimp
2 medium-size, soft-ripe avocados
Bibb lettuce or dill sprigs
Lemon wedges

Sprinkle gelatine over ½ cup of the broth. Simmer rest in saucepan with bay leaf 5 to 10 minutes. Add gelatine and stir until dissolved. Blend in salt, dried dill, vinegar, lemon juice, Tabasco and shrimp. Remove bay leaf and chill aspic to consistency of jellied consommé. Halve avocados lengthwise; remove seed and skin. Place on chilled salad plates, in nest of lettuce or fresh dill if you like. Heap with shrimp aspic. Garnish each with a lemon wedge. Makes 4 servings.

SALADE NICOISE

The bounty of sea and land mingle beautifully in this colorful salad from southern France. It varies with chef or home cook and may include more tuna and assorted cooked vegetables. This version was garnered in Nice on a recent trip.

1 to 2 heads Boston lettuce
2 cans (6½ to 7 ounces each) tuna
1 green or red sweet pepper, thinly sliced in rings
1 sweet red onion, peeled and thinly sliced in rings
1 young cucumber, peeled and thinly sliced
12 cherry tomatoes, halved

3 hard-cooked eggs, quartered
12 Mediterranean-type black olives
8 anchovy fillets, drained and chopped
1 clove garlic, crushed
1 teaspoon Dijon prepared mustard
⅔ cup Sauce Vinaigrette*

Half fill large shallow salad bowl with small center leaves lettuce. Drain tuna and break into big chunks. Nestle with rest of ingredients down to but not including anchovies in attractive groups on top of lettuce. It makes a pretty picture. Blend anchovies, garlic and mustard into vinaigrette; drizzle a few spoonfuls over salad. Cover with saran film and chill about 30 minutes. At serving time, present salad to guests untossed. Pour dressing over it, toss gently and serve on chilled salad plates. Makes 6 servings.

BUFFET SALAD NIÇOISE

On a large platter mound 2 cups French Potato Salad.* Outline with small lettuce leaves. Gently mix 2 cups cooked green beans with the tuna, onion, green pepper, black olives and half the dressing of preceding Salade Niçoise.* Omit cucumber. Heap in mound over potato salad. Garnish with cherry tomatoes and eggs. Drizzle salad with rest of dressing. Makes 8 to 10 servings.

THE ORIGINAL PALACE COURT SALAD

In their day, the chefs of the San Francisco Palace Hotel have originated many fabulous dishes. This is one of them and still a great luncheon specialty there.

Purchase the large meaty artichoke bottoms, in glass or can, at a fancy food shop unless you're pretty adept at trimming and de-choking an artichoke to get at its meaty heart. For each salad, place a ½ inch thick slice of large beefsteak tomato on 9-inch salad plate. Circle tomato with a thick border of shredded iceberg lettuce. Finely chop hard-cooked eggs and sprinkle thickly in a golden halo immediately around tomato slice. Press into 3-ounce aspic molds a salad of chicken, lobster, crab, shrimp or tuna mixed with celery, mayonnaise and your favorite seasoning. Turn carefully onto artichoke bottom, then set on top of tomato. Top with a bright round of pimiento. Serve with Louis Dressing.*

HERRING SALAD, STOCKHOLM
Sillsalad

A typical and expected part of a smörgåsbord . . . in fact no decent one would be caught without it!

1 jar (6 ounces) matjes,
  pickled or Bismarck herring
  (approximately ¾ cup
  chopped)
¼ cup diced onion
⅓ cup diced, cold boiled
  potato
2 tablespoons diced dill
  gherkin
⅓ cup diced apple
½ cup diced Vinegar Beets*
½ cup diced cooked ham or
  veal, optional

3 tablespoons pickled beet
  juice or vinegar
1 tablespoon water
1 tablespoon sugar
1 teaspoon prepared mustard
1 to 2 hard-cooked eggs
Lettuce leaves
Parsley or fresh dill
1 cup dairy sour cream
3 tablespoons pickled beet
  juice, for dressing

Dice herring fillets. Carefully mix with other diced ingredients; remember flavors should blend, but ingredients should not mash. Combine beet juice or vinegar, water, sugar and mustard. Pour dressing over fish mixture and gently stir it in. Lightly oil a 3½- or 4-cup mold and pack salad in. Chill 4 hours or more. Prepare hard-cooked eggs and chill; cut in wedges or dice whites and sieve yolks. Before serving unmold salad on lettuce leaves on a chilled platter. Garnish with wedges of eggs leaning into base of salad or scatter rows of diced whites and sieved yolks over salad mound. Add a sprig or two of greenery. Serve with a sauce boat filled with a blend of sour cream and beet juice. Makes 6 servings as a salad or 12 for smörgåsbord.

CRAB SALAD LOUIS

First made at the Olympic Club in Seattle, with Dungeness or perhaps Alaskan King crab, this unbeatable luncheon favorite is now made everywhere with every kind of shellfish. The season and location can determine your recipe.

1½ pounds lump crab meat	*Butter lettuce*
(or shrimp or lobster)	*4 medium tomatoes, peeled*
1 cup chopped celery	*4 hard-cooked eggs*
½ cup mayonnaise	*Louis Dressing**
Lemon juice	*Lemon wedges, ripe olives,*
White pepper	*avocado slices*

Pick over crab meat removing any bits of shell. Flake and mix gently with celery and enough mayonnaise to moisten, about ½ cup. Season with lemon juice and a little white pepper. Arrange lettuce on 4 large salad plates and heap with mounds of crab. Top each with a crab leg, if available, and surround with quartered tomatoes and hard-cooked eggs. Cover with saran film and chill at least 30 minutes before serving. Top each salad with a spoonful of Louis dressing, serve rest in a sauce bowl. Garnish plates with lemon wedges, ripe olives and avocado slices. Makes 4 jumbo luncheons.

Serve with French bread or hard rolls and a chilled dry white wine.

BLENDER TOMATO ASPIC

Wonderful to make and serve when tomatoes are red-ripe, bursting with sweet flavor and abundant.

2 *pounds red-ripe tomatoes,*
  peeled and chunked
1 *small onion, peeled and*
  chunked
1 *bay leaf, crumbled*
1 *teaspoon dried dill*
1½ *teaspoons salt*
½ *clove garlic*
2 *tablespoons unflavored*
  gelatine

⅓ *cup cold water*
2 *tablespoons vinegar or*
  lemon juice
1 *teaspoon sugar*
Crisp *salad greens*
Cucumber Dressing* *or*
  cottage cheese, optional

Place in blender (in two batches if necessary) tomatoes, onion, bay leaf, dill, salt and garlic. Whizz until puréed, about 10 seconds. Strain. Sprinkle gelatine over water and vinegar in metal cup and set in pan of hot water over low heat to melt. Stir into purée. Add sugar. Pour into 1-quart mold rinsed in cold water. Chill until firm. Unmold and garnish with salad greens. Serve with cucumber dressing or cottage cheese. Makes 4 to 5 servings.

CUCUMBER DRESSING

Stir into 1 cup dairy sour cream: seasoned salt† and pepper to taste, 2 teaspoons Maggi seasoning.† Chill. Just before serving, blend in 1 peeled, finely chopped and drained cucumber.

TART TOMATO MOLD

Here's an unbelievable combination for which we thank the Carmel, California, Crosbys. A strawberry-flavored gelatin, canned stewed tomatoes and lots of lemon . . . brilliant and bitey . . . it's the perfect accompaniment for game or pork.

1 can (14½ ounces) stewed
  tomatoes
1 package strawberry-flavored
  gelatin
2 to 3 tablespoons lemon
  juice

Lettuce leaves
½ cup Mayonnaise* and
  2 tablespoons Sauce
  Vinaigrette* or ½ cup
  sour cream

Strain tomatoes; reserve juice. In a small saucepan bring tomato juice to boil. Dissolve gelatin in it. Put tomatoes and other vegetables (from can) in chopping bowl; chop fine. Combine vegetables and gelatin mixture. Proportion lemon juice to suit your taste and food it will accompany; add lemon juice to mixture. Lightly oil 4 or 6 individual molds; pour salad into them. Chill 4 hours. Unmold each on chilled plate and lettuce leaves. Serve a sauce boat of mayonnaise thinned with sauce vinaigrette or simply sour cream, whichever appeals. Makes 4 to 6 servings.

AVOCADO MOUSSE PICANTE

Avocado must be soft for this and ripened to its full creamy texture and flavor. A superb dish for a luncheon or buffet with crisp rolls and a fruit dessert.

2 envelopes unflavored gelatine
2 cups cold chicken broth
1/4 cup lemon juice
2 tablespoons red wine vinegar
2 tablespoons minced green onion
2 to 3 soft-ripe avocados
2 teaspoons salt (approximately)

1/4 to 1/2 teaspoon salsa jalapeña or Mexican hot sauce†
1/3 cup mayonnaise
1 cup heavy cream, whipped
Romaine and crab legs or small tomatoes

Sprinkle gelatine over cold broth and stir over low heat until melted. Add lemon juice, vinegar and onion. Chill until cold but still liquid. Halve, seed and peel avocados; sieve or mash with fork, then beat until smooth and creamy. Measure 2 cups and blend into the cold aspic. Season with part of the salt and hot sauce, then blend in mayonnaise. Taste and add more seasoning as needed. Chill until thick but not set. Fold in whipped cream. Pour into 6-cup ring or mold and cover with saran film. Chill until set, 4 hours or more. Unmold on chilled plate and garnish with romaine spears and crab legs or peeled tomatoes, halved. Makes 8 to 10 servings.

CUCUMBER VELVET

Cool, pale and creamy with a delicate flavor.

2 cups peeled, seeded, diced
  cucumber (3 to 4 medium)
Salt
½ teaspoon sugar
3 envelopes unflavored gelatine
1 cup cold water
¼ cup white wine vinegar
2 tablespoons coarsely cut
  fresh mint leaves

2 slices onion, coarsely cut
⅓ cup parsley leaves, stripped
  of stems
1½ cups dairy sour cream
¼ cup mayonnaise
¼ teaspoon Tabasco sauce,
  or to taste
Fluted cucumber slices, fresh
  dill or mint sprigs

Sprinkle cucumber lightly with salt and the sugar; let stand 20 minutes. In saucepan, sprinkle gelatine over cold water and vinegar. Stir over low heat until gelatine is dissolved. Add 1 teaspoon salt and the mint leaves. Drain cucumber; place in blender with onion and parsley. Whizz until puréed. Pour in liquid gelatine and blend a few seconds, until smooth. Tiny green flecks of parsley and mint are still evident. Refrigerate, or quick-chill in freezer about 30 minutes, until thick and heavy, but not set. Beat in sour cream and mayonnaise. Season with Tabasco and a little more salt if needed. Pour into 1-quart mold; cover and chill until set, 3 to 4 hours. Unmold on chilled plate and garnish with thin cucumber slices and bouquets of dill or mint. Makes 6 servings.

FRUIT MOLD ROSE

A very subtle blending of color, flavor and bouquet. Because the base of this salad is rosé wine, it complements any dish . . . meat, fish or poultry.

2 envelopes unflavored gelatine
¼ cup sugar
¼ teaspoon salt
1½ cups boiling water
2 tablespoons lemon juice
1 teaspoon grated lemon peel
1⅔ cups rosé wine[1]
5 drops red food coloring
1 can (11 ounces) mandarin orange sections

1 can (8¾ ounces) grapefruit sections
½ cup diced unpeeled apple
½ cup chopped dates
¼ cup finely diced celery
Lettuce leaves
Mayonnaise*

Mix gelatine, sugar and salt in a large bowl. Add water; stir until gelatine has dissolved. Stir in lemon juice, grated peel, wine and coloring. Chill in refrigerator until syrupy and almost set. Drain orange and grapefruit sections; dice them. Add to apple, dates and celery and stir into gelatine. Lightly oil a 6-cup ring mold; pour in salad mixture. Chill 4 hours or more. Unmold on bed of lettuce leaves on chilled platter. Serve salad with mayonnaise. Makes 6 servings.

[1] If rosé wine is unavailable, pink chablis may be substituted.

MINTED MELON RING

A timeless cool combination—melons and mint—in a do-ahead ring of sparkling orange jelly.

2 envelopes unflavored gelatine
⅔ cup sugar
2 cups orange juice
¼ cup chopped mint leaves
½ cup fresh lemon juice
1 tray ice cubes (16 to 20 cubes)
Green food coloring, optional

3 cups mixed melon balls or cubes (cantaloupe, honeydew, Cranshaw or Persian)
½ cup seedless green grapes
Honey Coconut Dressing*
Red watermelon sticks, optional

Combine gelatine, sugar, 1 cup orange juice and mint in saucepan. Stirring constantly, heat to boiling over low heat. Remove from heat and add lemon juice, remaining cup orange juice and ice cubes. Stir several minutes until ice is melted and gelatine thickens (scoop out mint before it completely thickens and tint pale green, if you wish). Remove any unmelted ice. Gently fold in melon and grapes (try for a contrast of colors in the melon mixture). Turn into wet 6-cup mold. Cover and chill until set, 4 hours or more. Unmold on chilled plate and garnish with mint leaves and sticks of red watermelon, if you wish. Serve with honey coconut dressing. Makes 8 servings.

HONEY COCONUT DRESSING

Blend 2 tablespoons honey, lemon juice to taste and ¼ cup flaked coconut into 1 cup dairy sour cream. Makes about 1¼ cups.

ORANGE SALAD ROSEMARY

Peel 4 large seedless oranges removing all white membrane. Wrap in saran film and chill. Line 4 salad plates with lettuce leaves. On board, thinly slice each orange crosswise with sharp knife. Lift onto plates keeping shapes intact. Separate slices slightly in accordion effect. Drench with ¼ cup Honey Lemon Dressing* spiked with a pinch of crumbled rosemary leaves.

ICED FRUIT SALAD

If Weights and Measures are a problem, how about a lovely salad that tastes like it's loaded with creamy calories, and isn't.

5 tablespoons flour
⅓ cup table sugar
   replacement
2 teaspoons salt
½ teaspoons paprika
Few grains cayenne
4 egg yolks, well beaten
1⅓ cups skim milk
2 tablespoons safflower oil
¾ cup lemon juice
⅔ cup plain yogurt
6 tablespoons honey

1 envelope whipped topping
   mix
½ cup skim milk
2 cans (16 ounces each)
   dietetic fruit salad, drained
1 can (16 ounces) dietetic
   crushed pineapple, drained
Lettuce leaves
Fresh blueberries, raspberries
   or strawberries
Fresh mint sprigs
Pineapple Salad Dressing*

Combine flour, table sugar replacement, salt, paprika and cayenne in top of double boiler. Blend egg yolks with 1⅓ cups milk and stir gradually into dry ingredients; cook until thick, stirring constantly. Add oil and lemon juice; blend until smooth. Cook a few minutes longer until rethickened. Pour into bowl; cool it. Add yogurt and blend in carefully. Add honey. Make whipped topping mix (omit vanilla) with ½ cup skim milk. Fold into salad mixture, then drained fruits. Pour into refrigerator trays or two 8-inch square pans. Freeze about 4 hours. Before serving cut into squares and place each square on a bed of lettuce, or serve, unmolded on a large platter. Garnish with berries and mint. Makes 12 servings. If all is not to be used at once, cover containers and put back for future use. It may be served with or without the dressing.

Pineapple Salad Dressing

2 egg yolks, well beaten
2 tablespoons flour
1 cup dietetic pineapple
   juice

1 envelope whipped topping
   mix
½ cup skim milk

Use a whisk to combine yolks with flour in top part of double boiler. Add juice and cook until thickened, stirring constantly. Remove and cool. Make whipped topping mix (omit vanilla) with ½ cup skim milk. Fold into pineapple mixture and chill. Makes about 2½ cups.

VEGETABLES A LA GRECQUE

Practically every vegetable that comes to mind is cool and inviting when cooked and chilled in this lively Greek marinade. Vary it and the vegetables to suit your own tastes—more oil, less lemon or vice versa and different herbs. *One* or *all* the vegetables listed may be used—you can think of others—but try for a contrast in shapes, textures, flavors and colors. The marinade is sufficient for 5 to 6 cups vegetables, cooked 2 cups at a time.

Greek Marinade:

½ teaspoon dried thyme leaves, crushed	4 sprigs parsley
½ teaspoon coriander seeds	2 cloves garlic, sliced
½ teaspoon fennel seeds	3 cups water
½ teaspoon marjoram	¾ cup olive oil
1 bay leaf, broken	½ cup fresh lemon juice
12 whole black peppercorns	1 tablespoon tarragon vinegar
2 whole cloves	1 teaspoon salt

Tie herbs, seeds, spices, parsley and garlic loosely in cheesecloth. Combine remaining ingredients in deepish 2-quart saucepan; add herb bag and bring to boil. Cover loosely and simmer 15 minutes. Press bag to release flavors occasionally. Makes 1 quart.

Prepare any combination of vegetables from those below; simmer in marinade as directed for each. Vegetables that require the same cooking time may be cooked together. When they are just crisp-tender, remove with slotted spoon to bowl or refrigerator dish. When all are cooked, remove herb bag and pour hot marinade over vegetables. Cool, loosely covered, then cover tightly and chill overnight. Arrange attractively in neat groups on serving platter; drizzle with marinade and garnish with lemon wedges. Or serve as salad platter on lettuce with tomato wedges, olives, anchovies and sliced hard-cooked eggs.

Mushrooms—Wash 2 cups fresh mushrooms quickly and drop into simmering marinade. Cook 5 to 8 minutes.

Green Peppers—Halve and seed 2 large peppers; cut into 1-inch strips. Simmer 8 to 12 minutes, *only* until crisp-tender.

Cucumbers—Slice unpeeled cucumbers in ¼-inch rounds or cut into sticks about 4 inches long. Simmer 6 to 10 minutes.

Celery—Slice celery stalks on a slant into 1-inch crescents. Simmer about 10 minutes.

Carrots—Scrape tender young carrots and slice on a slant into ½-inch ovals or cut into quarters lengthwise. Simmer 10 to 12 minutes.

Okra—Select whole young okra pods no more than 3 inches long. Simmer until just tender, about 10 minutes.

Artichoke Hearts—Trim fresh young artichokes (the 2- to 3-inch size that's all edible is usually found only in Italian markets). Simmer about 15 minutes. Simmer frozen artichoke hearts 5 to 8 minutes *only*.

Green Beans—Trim fresh tender young beans and simmer whole until crisp-tender 15 to 20 minutes. Or slice beans on slant into 2-inch pieces and simmer 10 to 15 minutes. Simmer canned or frozen whole beans 6 to 8 minutes only.

ASPARAGUS MIMOSA

2 pounds fresh asparagus
2 hard-cooked eggs
*Sauce Vinaigrette**

Bend asparagus stalks backward near bottom to snap off tough ends and remove scales with knife tip. Wash asparagus; tie in bundles, if you wish. Drop into large wide kettle containing enough boiling salted water to cover it. Cook rapidly, uncovered, 8 to 10 minutes, until just tender. Drain, plunge in cold water and drain on paper towels. Place in serving dish, cover with saran film and chill. About ½ hour before serving, chop egg whites finely and add to vinaigrette; pour over asparagus. At serving time, force egg yolks through sieve directly onto asparagus in wide band leaving tips uncovered. Makes 4 to 6 servings.

Bacon Mimosa

Sieve egg yolks over 4 slices crisp-cooked bacon, crumbled on piece of waxed paper. Add 1 tablespoon minced parsley. Sprinkle over dressed asparagus as above.

ASPARAGUS MAYONNAISE

Either cooked fresh asparagus or the canned jumbo white spears are delicious and elegant chilled and served with a fine mustardy mayonnaise.

Cook and chill 2 pounds asparagus as in Asparagus Mimosa,* or chill before opening 2 cans (about 1 pound each) jumbo white asparagus spears. Drain and arrange neatly on serving platter. Decorate with julienne strips pimiento. Serve with Mustard Mayonnaise.*

Mustard Mayonnaise

Blend into ⅔ cup mayonnaise, 1 to 2 teaspoons fresh lemon juice, 2 teaspoons Dijon mustard, 2 tablespoons cream and a pinch of nutmeg. Chill.

ARTICHOKES VINAIGRETTE

Serve elegantly as a separate course.

Tear off large outer leaves, trim stem and lay artichokes on board. With heavy French knife cut off 1 inch of leaves straight across top. Drop artichokes into large kettle of boiling salted water containing thick slice of lemon, 1 tablespoon salad oil. Cover loosely and boil briskly until tender, 20 to 40 minutes, depending on size. Remove from water and drain upside down. Cool and chill. for disposal of leaves. Serve small bowl of Sauce Vinaigrette* well Serve on special artichoke plate or large salad plate with room seasoned with Dijon mustard on side as dipping sauce.

SPLIT-IT ARTICHOKES

A whole globe artichoke is impressive, halves are more manageable and provide their own sauce bowl when choke is removed.

Lay chilled, cooked artichoke on board and split lengthwise into halves with one sharp cut of heavy French knife. With teaspoon, scoop out the fuzzy, thistle-like choke just above the heart or artichoke bottom. Place halves on salad plates and fill with one of the seasoned mayonnaise dressings (in Sauces chapter) or this delectable sauce as dip for leaves.

Curry Sauce—For 4 large halves, blend 1 teaspoon curry powder, ½ teaspoon Worcestershire sauce, few drops grated onion into ½ cup mayonnaise.

MASKED CAULIFLOWER

An unusual sauce of shrimp and avocado frosts a snowy head of cauliflower handsomely and effectively.

1 large head cauliflower	1 soft-ripe avocado
Salt	1 green onion, sliced
1 slice lemon	1 can (about 4½ ounces)
2 tablespoons Sauce	tiny shrimp
Vinaigrette*	½ cup mayonnaise
2 tablespoons fresh lemon juice	2 tomatoes, peeled and sliced

Trim cauliflower leaving some of the tender green leaves around base. Drop whole into large pot of boiling salted water with slice of lemon. Cook briskly only until crisp-tender, 12 to 15 minutes. Drain, and sprinkle with vinaigrette. Cool, cover with saran film and chill. Put lemon juice in blender. Halve and deseed avocado. Set one half aside for garnish; wrap in saran film. Peel and dice remaining avocado into blender; whizz until smooth, a few seconds. Add onion and two-thirds of shrimp, drained. Whizz until smooth. Mix with mayonnaise. Season with a little salt if needed. Just before serving, place cauliflower on chilled plate and frost with sauce. Scatter rest of drained shrimp over top. Ring with crosswise crescents of avocado and halved tomato slices. Makes 4 to 6 servings.

CAPONATA

Our adaptation of a colorful vegetable mélange served in New York's popular Trattoria in the Pan Am building. In Italy, this is often suggested as part of the antipasto. We like it as a vegetable with grilled fish or meat, or as a full meal with cheese and French or Armenian bread.

½ cup olive and peanut oil, combined (approximately)

1 large unpeeled eggplant, cut in 1-inch cubes

1 large onion, sliced

2 large green peppers, deseeded and cut in strips

2 stalks celery, thinly sliced

1 can (12 ounces) Italian pear-shaped tomatoes

1 large clove garlic, minced

1 teaspoon sugar

1½ teaspoons salt

Freshly ground pepper to taste

½ pound black and green olives, mixed[2]

2 tablespoons chopped parsley

2 tablespoons capers and juice

2 tablespoons lemon juice or wine vinegar

In large heavy pan, heat about half the oil and add eggplant. Cook and stir gently until tender but shapely, 5 to 10 minutes. Remove and drain. Heat rest of oil and add onion, peppers and celery. Cook, stirring frequently, until onion is golden, about 5 minutes. Add tomatoes, garlic, sugar, salt and pepper; cook gently about 15 minutes, until vegetables are cooked down but still have shape and identity. Lightly stir in eggplant, olives, parsley and capers. Cook a few minutes longer. Cool. Cover with saran film and refrigerate. Flavors improve if chilled overnight. Remove from refrigerator 10 minutes before serving. Add lemon juice or vinegar to taste. Makes 6 servings.

[2] Italians usually make this with the wrinkled black Italian or Greek olives. We used the more available California ripe olives.

Plate No. 3— Serenely cold and beautiful, ready in the refrigerator when you are. *Chicken Breasts en Gelée* (p. 75), *Jambon Persillé* with *Mustard Fruit Mayonnaise* (p. 92) and *Dilly Tuna in Jellied Egg Ring* (p. 97). Photograph by Robert E. Coates, courtesy of *Woman's Day* magazine.

CHAPTER VI

Sauces, Dressings and Relishes

"The sauce makes the dish," we found ourselves saying many times as we tasted and tested our way through the recipes in this book. In most cases we have placed the accompanying sauce with the particular recipe it enhances. And you will find more sauces elsewhere than those in this small chapter.[1] But, mayonnaise and vinaigrette and their more popular variations, which seem to go with so many cold foods—main dishes as well as salads and vegetables—and other basic, go-with-all sauces or dressings, we've placed in this chapter.

The same is true with some of our special relishes and pickled dishes. A number are suggested throughout the book with the food they accent best. Others, like Brandied Peaches or Pink Pickled Eggs, that seem to provide just the right sparkle and zip for a number of dishes we've put here.

[1] Other sauces may be found in the Appetizers, Entrées, Salads and Desserts chapters, or by consulting the Index.

MAYONNAISE

Mayonnaise is the basis of dozens of marvelous sauces and limitless in its uses with cold foods. Without it we can't imagine what our book would be like. Most of our recipes were made with a fine quality commercial mayonnaise which we find hard to beat. But there's satisfaction and fun in making a batch of mayonnaise with your own special seasonings and spices. In our opinion, it sort of ranks with the pleasure derived from baking a loaf of bread from scratch or cranking a freezerful of homemade ice cream.

For the occasions when you wish to make your own, here's a basic recipe for hand-whipped or mixer-made and another for the speedy blender type.

2 egg yolks, at room temperature

½ teaspoon dry mustard, or to taste

½ teaspoon salt, or to taste

1 tablespoon vinegar or lemon juice

1 cup salad or olive oil (or a mixture of the two)

White pepper

Seasonings, ad lib

Rinse mixing bowl or bowl of electric mixer with hot water. Dry. Beat egg yolks with wire whisk or in mixer until they are thick, about 1 minute. Beat in mustard, salt and 1 teaspoon vinegar or lemon juice. Gradually, drop by drop, beat in ¼ cup oil. With a mixer this is no problem. With a wire whisk, it's fairly easy if you brace the bowl so it won't slip around or rock, and drip in the oil with one hand while manning the whisk with the other. By this time, the egg and oil will have formed a creamy emulsion. You can now beat in another teaspoon vinegar and the rest of the oil in a fine stream. Beat constantly, but stop now and then to see if all the oil is being absorbed. When all the oil is beaten in, sauce will be thick, smooth and satiny looking. Beat in last teaspoon vinegar. Taste and season with white pepper, more vinegar or lemon juice and herbs or whatever seasonings you desire. Cover tightly and refrigerate. Makes a generous cup delicious mayonnaise.

BLENDER MAYONNAISE

Egg yolks only and lime juice make this blender mayonnaise different from others.

2 egg yolks
½ teaspoon salt
½ teaspoon dry mustard
Few grains cayenne
½ teaspoon Worcestershire
 sauce

3 tablespoons lime or lemon
 juice
1½ cups salad oil, or less

Put egg yolks, seasonings, Worcestershire, lime juice and ¼ cup oil in blender. Cover and whizz to blend on slow speed. Remove cover and add a steady stream of oil with motor running. Use rubber spatula, if necessary, to keep ingredients flowing to processing blades. Blend only until very thick and smooth; use less oil if it thickens quickly. Makes about 1 pint.

SAUCE REMOULADE

A favorite with shrimp but great with any chilled seafood.

Add to 1 cup mayonnaise: 1 clove garlic, crushed, 1 tablespoon prepared mustard, ¼ teaspoon dry mustard, 1 tablespoon each capers and minced parsley, 1 teaspoon dried tarragon, 1 teaspoon anchovy paste, 1 minced hard-cooked egg. Mix well and chill. Makes generous cup.

MAYONNAISE CHANTILLY

A light, fluffy dressing for fruit salads and molds, cole slaw and, surprisingly, for many cold fish dishes.

Whip ½ cup heavy cream and fold into 1 cup mayonnaise. Gently stir in 1 tablespoon lemon juice, 2 teaspoons grated lemon peel. Makes about 2 cups.

JELLIED MAYONNAISE

Also called *mayonnaise colée* or *mayonnaise chaud froid*, this recipe is a switch from the traditional. More delicate, we think. Use it to mask cold poached fish, chicken breasts, or sliced chicken or turkey.

1 envelope unflavored gelatine	1 cup mayonnaise
1/4 cup cold chicken broth or water	2 tablespoons lemon juice
	1/2 cup heavy cream, whipped

Sprinkle gelatine over chicken broth and dissolve by stirring over hot water. Cool slightly and stir into mayonnaise. Blend in lemon juice. Chill a few minutes if mayonnaise has thinned, then fold in whipped cream. Light accents of curry powder, mustard, grated lemon or orange peels may be added, depending on foods to be masked. Makes 2 cups.

LOUIS DRESSING

Lusty pink dressing for cold fish, particularly shellfish. Some chefs prefer catsup, but our research indicates the original used chili sauce.

1 cup mayonnaise	2 tablespoons lemon juice, or to taste
1/3 cup chili sauce	White pepper
1 tablespoon grated onion	
1 tablespoon minced parsley	
1/2 teaspoon Worcestershire sauce	

Mix all ingredients. Cover and chill if desired. Makes about 1½ cups.

DILL CREAM MAYONNAISE

2 cups mayonnaise

2 tablespoons chopped fresh
    dill or about 2 teaspoons
    dried dill

1 tablespoon Dijon mustard

2 tablespoons chopped chives

Lemon juice to taste

½ cup heavy cream, whipped

Combine mayonnaise and dill, mustard, chives and lemon juice. Chill 2 hours before serving. Fold in whipped cream. Makes about 3 cups.

SAUCE VERTE

Classic green mayonnaise with some piquant additions.

½ cup watercress leaves

12 young spinach leaves

4 green onions, chopped

¼ cup chopped parsley

1 tablespoon fresh tarragon
    leaves or 2 teaspoons
    dried tarragon

1 cup dairy sour cream

1 pint mayonnaise

Salt, cayenne pepper, Tabasco

Lemon juice

Drop watercress, spinach, green onions in boiling water for a few seconds. Drain, rinse in cold water and blot dry. Purée in blender with parsley, tarragon and sour cream. Add to mayonnaise. Season lightly with salt, cayenne, Tabasco and lemon juice. Makes generous 3 cups sauce.

CHUTNEY DRESSING

Pungent, yet with a lingering hint of sweet. Great with ham, tongue and poultry dishes.

1 cup mayonnaise
1 cup dairy sour cream
1/4 cup chopped chutney

1/2 teaspoon curry powder
Pinch each dry mustard and
  powdered ginger

Combine all ingredients and chill. Makes generous 2 cups.

RED ROQUEFORT DRESSING

Here's taste and color that's almost psychedelic . . . the blend of flaming red pimiento and robust Roquefort.

1 can (4 ounces) pimientos,
  drained
1 1/4 ounces (2 tablespoons)
  Roquefort cheese
1/4 cup vinegar

1/3 cup salad oil
1/2 teaspoon sugar
1/2 teaspoon salt
1/4 teaspoon dry mustard
1/4 teaspoon pepper

Put ingredients in electric blender. Cover and whizz it on high speed until puréed and blended. Makes a little more than 1 cup.

WATERCRESS DRESSING

In the crystal clear springs surrounding Pearl Harbor, watercress grows to an enormous size . . . so has this dressing's popularity. Try it on wedges of lettuce or as a sauce for fish.

1 bunch watercress, regular
  size
1 clove garlic, crushed
1 cup mayonnaise

1/2 teaspoon salt
Pepper to taste
1 tablespoon lemon juice

Put ingredients in blender; whizz until smooth. Chill. Makes about 1 1/2 cups.

SAUCE VINAIGRETTE

Call it French dressing, *sauce vinaigrette* or whatever you wish, in the country of its origin it means simply a light mixture of oil, wine vinegar, salt and pepper. There, it's a basic for the *salades* of fresh greens, but serves dozens of other purposes as well—a marinade or sauce for cold meats and fish and every cooked vegetable you can name. The usual proportions are three parts oil to one of vinegar or lemon juice, but vary it to suit your own tastes and uses. And season, ad lib with garlic, mustard, various herbs and spices.

To clarify the names and labels on bottled dressings frequently used as well as the various dressings served by many restaurants, this may be helpful. Those called "oil and vinegar" and "Italian" more closely resemble the French vinaigrette than the majority named "French dressing." Often the Italian is more highly seasoned, usually with garlic, an assortment of herbs and, occasionally, an Italian cheese.

¾ teaspoon salt
1 clove garlic, crushed with
* the salt, optional*
Pinch dry mustard, optional
3 to 4 tablespoons wine
* vinegar*

¾ cup salad oil or olive oil
* (or a mixture)*
Generous grinding black
* pepper*

You may combine all ingredients and shake vigorously in jar until blended, but we like to beat it with a wire whisk to a soft creamy emulsion. The flavor seems richer, mellower. With whisk, beat salt, garlic, if used, and mustard into vinegar, then beat in oil, in small portions, until sauce is smooth and lightly thickened. Season with pepper. Use at once or store in bottle and shake vigorously before using. Makes 1 cup.

HERB VINAIGRETTE

Beat 1 tablespoon Dijon mustard into vinegar before adding oil. Season with 1 teaspoon each chopped fresh chives, tarragon, chervil and parsley (or 1 teaspoon mixed dried herbs).

Lemon Tarragon Dressing

Replace wine vinegar with 1 tablespoon tarragon wine vinegar, 3 tablespoons lemon juice in basic Sauce Vinaigrette.* Season with 2 to 3 teaspoons chopped fresh tarragon or 1 teaspoon crumbled dried tarragon leaves.

Custom Vinaigrette

Add to Sauce Vinaigrette* 1 teaspoon curry powder for fruit and chicken salads; 1 tablespoon chopped fresh basil (or 1 teaspoon dried) for tomato salads; 1 to 2 tablespoons chopped fresh dill or dried dill weed to taste for sliced cucumbers; 2 tablespoons each chopped onion and parsley, 1 tablespoon prepared mustard for potato salads.

SAUCE GRIBICHE

A colorful, piquant sauce for cold meats, asparagus, artichoke hearts, green beans.

2 hard-cooked eggs
½ teaspoon salt
¾ teaspoon dry mustard
Generous grinding black
  pepper
⅓ cup vinegar
1 cup salad oil

2 tablespoons chopped sour
  pickles
2 tablespoons chopped capers
1 tablespoon mixed chopped
  parsley, tarragon and chervil
1 tablespoon chopped scallions
  or green onions

Mash egg yolks with the salt, mustard and pepper. Alternately beat in, little by little, the vinegar and oil. Stir in chopped egg whites, pickles, capers, herbs and scallions. Makes 1½ cups.

SPICY TOMATO DRESSING

Lively flavor, low in calories. Seasoned tomato sauce replaces part of the salad oil.

½ cup tomato sauce	Generous dash dry mustard
3 tablespoons vinegar	2 teaspoons minced onion
½ teaspoon salt	1 clove garlic, crushed
½ teaspoon Worcestershire sauce	6 tablespoons salad oil

Combine in jar and shake vigorously. Chill and shake again before using. Makes about 1 cup.

CELERY SEED DRESSING

Crystal clear, sweet and seedy . . . a great dressing for fruit salads.

1 tablespoon white corn syrup	½ teaspoon salt
⅓ cup sugar	½ cup vinegar
1 tablespoon paprika	1⅓ cups salad oil
1 teaspoon dry mustard	1 tablespoon celery seeds

Boil all ingredients together, except oil and celery seed, for 2 minutes. Let cool. Add salad oil slowly, beating constantly or place cooled mixture in blender and add oil gradually, with motor running. Add celery seed last; beat in, whizz in or simply stir in. Let dressing chill overnight before serving. Makes about 1 pint.

ANCHOVY DRESSING

Try this on the Antipasto Salad* or a tossed green . . . you'll like.

¼ cup tarragon wine vinegar
½ cup salad oil
½ cup evaporated milk
½ clove garlic, crushed
½ teaspoon salt
½ teaspoon dry mustard

¼ teaspoon pepper
1 slice (¼ inch) medium
  onion
¼ cup chopped parsley
2 cans (2 ounces each)
  anchovies, with oil

Put all ingredients in blender, including anchovy oil. Cover and whizz it, until dressing is smooth. Chill. Makes about 1½ cups.

LEMON CREAM DRESSING

Believe it or not, this has fewer calories than vinaigrette or mayonnaise. A French favorite often used on delicate greens such as limestone lettuce, butter lettuce and the like.

½ cup heavy cream
2 tablespoons lemon juice

¼ teaspoon salt
Dash white pepper

Blend together and pour over greens. Makes enough dressing for about 6 cups lettuce.

HONEY LEMON DRESSING

Instant light dressing for fruit plates, fruit cups.

Combine in jar equal amounts of honey and fresh lemon juice. Cover and shake vigorously until well blended. Chill and shake again before using. A few chopped mint leaves, fresh or dried herbs, poppy seeds or sesame seeds may be added.

Honey Lime Dressing:

Substitute fresh lime juice for the lemon juice.

Sherry Honey Dressing:

Use equal parts honey, lemon or lime juice and sherry. A bit of finely chopped chutney or preserved ginger makes a nice addition to this combination for some salads.

MUSTARD CREAM SAUCE

Sweet-sour and hot! Delectable with ham or tongue, some salmon dishes, cabbage and apple salads.

1 recipe Swedish Mustard Sauce*
1 cup dairy sour cream

Blend together and chill. Makes 2 cups.

PINK PICKLED EGGS

These pickled hard-cooked eggs will spoil you . . . they make the plain ones seem dull by comparison.

1 dozen hard-cooked eggs	*1 teaspoon pickling spices*
2 tablespoons sugar	*2 cups cider vinegar*
1 teaspoon salt	*½ cup water*
1 teaspoon celery seed	*Beet juice, optional*

Place peeled eggs in a quart jar. Add seasonings, celery seed and pickling spices to vinegar and water in a saucepan. Simmer about 10 minutes. Cool mixture and strain it. If you wish a pinky tint, add beet juice in desired amount. Pour pickling mixture over eggs. Seal and place in refrigerator for 2 to 3 days. Serve whole, halved or quartered any time or place you would normally use a hard-cooked egg.

CUCUMBER SALAD

Agurkesalat

Among Danish vegetables, this "salad" is one of the most popular. They use it as a companion to meats, a garnish to open sandwiches or as a cold table salad . . . at any meal except breakfast!

2 *large (8-inch) cucumbers*	¼ *teaspoon pepper*
½ *cup white wine vinegar*	2½ *tablespoons sugar*
¼ *cup water*	*Fresh parsley or dill*
½ *teaspoon salt*	

Plan to prepare these cucumbers no more than ½ hour ahead of serving; this ensures crispness. If rind is tender, peeling is unnecessary and the touch of green edging is pretty. If cucumbers are tough-skinned, peel first then score the length of each with the tines of a fork to create ridged effect. Slice as thinly as possible; pieces should be almost see-thru. Place them in serving dish. Combine other ingredients, except parsley or dill, to make dressing. Beat dressing to dissolve sugar. Pour over cucumbers. Sprinkle with chopped parsley or dill. Cover serving dish with saran film and chill in refrigerator. Before serving some liquid may be drained off, according to your use for the cucumbers. Makes 4 to 6 servings.

VINEGAR BEETS

Inlagd Rödbeta

Enjoy this traditional Scandinavian food as part of a salad, a relish or a vegetable side dish. Children and adults both like this vegetable.

Beets from 2 bunches, about
  3 to 4 cups sliced
Salt
½ cup vinegar
½ cup water
1 teaspoon salt

½ teaspoon freshly ground
  black pepper
3 cloves
1 bay leaf
¼ cup sugar

Prepare beets by boiling slowly in salted water for about 45 minutes, depending on size. (When cutting them for cooking, leave at least 1-inch stem on the beet . . . then they do not "bleed.") When beets are tender to a fork, remove and run cold water over them while in the pot in the sink. Slip off the skins and slice in rounds. Prepare dressing mixture, composed of vinegar, ½ cup water, seasonings, cloves, bay leaf and sugar. Pour over still hot beets. Refrigerate in a covered container 4 hours or overnight. Makes 6 to 8 servings.

JELLIED CRANBERRY RELISH

Your favorite raw cranberry relish blender-made into a colorful jelly.

2 envelopes unflavored gelatine
½ cup cold water
½ cup port wine
1½ cups sugar, or to taste
1 medium orange, cut in
  pieces and seeded

3 cups fresh cranberries,
  washed and picked over
½ cup walnuts, optional

Sprinkle gelatine over cold water in blender container. Let stand while you assemble other ingredients. Heat wine to boiling and pour into blender. Whizz at low speed until gelatine dissolves. Push any gelatine granules on sides of blender into mixture with rubber scraper. Add sugar and orange; whizz at high speed until orange is finely chopped. Add cranberries; whizz until berries are finely chopped. If used, add walnuts and whizz until coarsely chopped. Turn into pretty 4- to 5-cup mold or 8 small molds. Chill until firm, 4 hours or more. Makes 1 quart relish.

CRANBERRY CHUTNEY

1 cup sugar
1 onion, chopped
1 clove garlic, chopped
6 whole cloves
1 teaspoon cinnamon
2 cardamom seeds, peeled
   and crushed

Generous dash cayenne pepper
¼ teaspoon ground ginger
½ teaspoon salt
¼ cup vinegar
2 cups fresh cranberries
1 cup seedless raisins
⅓ cup brown sugar

Combine first 9 ingredients with 1 cup water; simmer 5 minutes. Add rest of ingredients and simmer gently 10 to 12 minutes. Serve chilled. Makes 2 pints.

GINGER MINT RELISH

Wonderful with turkey, ham or cold lamb!

1 cup washed, fresh mint
   leaves, packed
1½ cups dark raisins, rinsed
   and drained
¼-inch slice peeled fresh
   ginger root or 2 tablespoons
   chopped preserved ginger

¼ cup India pickle relish
1 teaspoon shredded orange
   peel
Few drops lemon or orange
   juice

Grind together mint leaves, raisins and ginger. Stir in pickle relish, orange peel and lemon or orange juice. Chill several hours before serving. Makes 1 pint.

BRANDIED PEACHES

Home-style copies of the expensive fruits found in gourmet food shops.

Drain into saucepan ½ cup syrup from 1 can (1 pound, 13 ounces) cling peach halves. Add 1 dozen whole cloves, ¼ cup sugar; simmer 5 minutes. Add peaches and heat to boiling again. Put fruit in glass jar. Add 1 tablespoon lemon juice, ½ cup brandy to syrup; pour hot over fruit. Cover tightly. Cool and refrigerate one week before using. Good as light dessert also. Makes 1½ pints.

CURRIED PEACHES

Quick bright accents for meat, salads or sandwiches.

Blend in saucepan ¾ teaspoon curry powder, 2 tablespoons sugar, 3 tablespoons wine vinegar, a little shredded lemon peel. Add 1 can (1 pound, 13 ounces) cling peach halves with syrup. Heat to boiling. Cover and cool. Refrigerate, covered, overnight. Makes 1½ pints.

CHAPTER VII

Sandwiches and
Smorrebrod ✑

Sandwiches have endured a good many refinements since they were simple rounds of bread that served as plates for food. In those days, the well heeled ate the food on top and left peasants with the soggy but nourishing bread underneath. Somewhere along the way, the Earl of Sandwich elevated the status of bread. He liked his card games uninterrupted, so in order to eat and play he devised the convenient two slices of bread with meat "sandwiched" between. And meanwhile, in Denmark, they cut down their bread needs to one thin slice, slathered it with butter or drippings and mounded it with all things edible.

It's a cinch to say that sandwiches have gained in popularity, everywhere. Single, double, triple deckers composed of everything and anything . . . even ice cream . . . have become a way of life. A school lunch box wouldn't be the same without sandwiches . . . nor would a picnic. Unexpected guests are easy to handle with a supply of cold cuts, canned goods and bread, and the breezy way to entertain at planned parties is . . . sandwiches.

The question is, in sandwiches, are you a Dagwood or a Dagmar? To delineate: a Dagwood *is* a sandwich, often casual, with more than one slice of bread clapping it together . . . a Dagmar is a true smørrebrød (buttered bread), open-faced and artistically laden.

This chapter should probably be called the Ad-lib section of our book, for, whichever kind you prefer, the combinations are endless and even leftovers are in good taste. Sandwiches are being invented daily, nightly too by some refrigerator-raiding Dagwoods. Smørrebrød has become a national dish and a national art in Denmark, and as expected, each year the list grows. The world-renowned

Oskar Davidsen's restaurant in Copenhagen has the distinction of a smørrebrød menu four feet long!

Sandwich-making can be easily done ahead of time, if sandwiches are wrapped in a cloth wrung out in cold water or dressed beautifully and secured in saran film, and refrigerated. Some sandwiches may be packaged and frozen. Smørrebrød is something else; these delicacies should not be made far ahead. Since there's no rooftop to hide the contents, neatness is essential. Next in importance is color and imagination. A good rule here is that hard and soft go together . . . for instance, liver paste goes well with toast or crisp bread and hard sausage is better on fresh wheat bread than a firm rye.

Good thinking for the ready-pantry is canned sardines, salmon, tuna and shrimp, and you can't miss with a jar of mayonnaise, horseradish and gherkins. Ready in the refrigerator should be some cheese, tomatoes, eggs, lemons, lettuce, watercress and cucumbers. Add to, or subtract; try our suggestions and invent some of your own. Feel free in this field, it's pretty hard to go wrong!

SMORREBROD

A variety of breads may be used. Pumpernickel rye bread should be cut about ⅛ inch thick. Danish wheat bread, similar to French bread but not as crusty, is usually cut between ¼ to ½ inch thick. Often their "French loaf" is toasted lightly to give it a little body for the soft toppings. It should never be buttered while hot. All bread used is to be well buttered.

Literally, whatever is "laid on" a slice of bread should cover it . . . the topping should hide *all* the foundation. In many cases smørrebrød makings are interchangeable. The examples given below are fairly standard in Denmark, but you will want to create a few of your own after you get the knack. If prepared ahead, and they usually are, cover all smørrebrød with saran film until serving time. Each recipe below makes 1 serving.

HOMEMADE LIVER PASTE
With Beets and Cucumber Salad

One of Denmark's most popular "everyday" sandwiches. The rich paste, accented with beet strips and cucumber rounds, has interesting flavor, color, texture and form.

1 slice pumpernickel bread,   *Slices Cucumber Salad,**
   or wheat toast   *drained*
Thick slices cold Liver Paste*
Strips plain or Vinegar Beets,*
   drained

Cover bread completely with liver paste slices. (For smørrebrød, a paste should not be spread, it should be sliced.) Decorate with beet strips and a row of cucumber slices.

CRAB SALAD

A light and thoroughly pleasant sandwich.

Crab meat, fresh cooked,   *Shredded lettuce*
   frozen or canned   *1 slice toasted wheat bread*
Mayonnaise   *Sliced hard-cooked egg*
Tarragon vinegar   *Tomato pieces*
Canned asparagus   *Spray fresh dill*

Mix crab meat pieces with mayonnaise which has been diluted with a small amount of vinegar. Add ½-inch cuts of asparagus and a little shredded lettuce. Cover bread with salad. Garnish with a slice of egg, a few pieces cut from tomato and dill spray.

CHICKEN SALAD WITH MUSHROOMS

A worldwide favorite with a Danish accent.

*Coarsely chopped roast or
  boiled chicken*
Mayonnaise
*Canned mushrooms with
  some liquid*

Shredded apple
1 slice pumpernickel bread
Chicken breast pieces
Mimosa egg garnish

Combine chopped chicken with mayonnaise. Add a few mushrooms; some shredded apple. If desired, thin mayonnaise with mushroom liquid. Cover bread with salad. Place a few large pieces of chicken on top; sprinkle with mimosa garnish.

TILSITER CHEESE
With Radish Rings

All smørrebrød have eye appeal, but not all are complicated works of art. Even the plain face of a cut of cheese becomes distinguished with some sliced radishes scattered across it . . . tastes good too!

1 slice pumpernickel bread
1 slice Tilsiter cheese or Swiss cheese
6 to 8 unpeeled radish slices

Cover bread with cheese. Slice radishes in varying sizes; place each round on top of cheese.

SMOKED TONGUE
With Italian Salad

Tongue is a Danish favorite, and especially paired with Italian Salad. Funny thing about *that* salad, it's called Italian but it has no connection with Italy . . . it is Danish Macaroni Salad* with carrots and peas added.

3 *very thin slices Beef Tongue* or Danish boiled ham*	*Italian Salad** *1 slice pumpernickel bread* *Parsley*

Spread each slice of tongue with a little salad and roll it. Place 3 rolls on top of bread. Garnish with parsley.

Italian Salad:

Delete ham from Danish Macaroni Salad* recipe. Add 1 can (8¼ ounces) diced carrots and peas (drained) to recipe; or 1 cup cooked fresh carrots and peas may be substituted, if preferred. The vegetable quantity is also a matter of taste.

LOBSTER WITH CURRY MAYONNAISE

Lobster salad is comparatively easy and you will like the taste of this mayonnaise with it.

Lobster, fresh cooked, frozen or canned *Mayonnaise* *Curry powder, to taste*	*1 slice toasted wheat bread* *Sliced tomato* *Finely chopped fresh dill*

Combine chunks of lobster with mayonnaise that is blended and seasoned with curry powder. Cover bread with salad. Garnish with thin slice of tomato and chopped dill.

CORNETS OF HAM AND FOIE GRAS

Ham can get pretty exotic when spread with Strasbourg pâté de foie gras, and by rights it should have the best bread and ham you can find.

*Strasbourg pâté de foie gras
or a good liver pâté made
with truffles*

*3 square slices boiled ham
1 slice wheat bread
Crystal Aspic**

Spread pâté on each ham slice; roll into cone shape. Turn open edge side down and place on bread slice. Garnish, in and around, with chopped aspic. It is particularly good with wine flavoring the aspic.

FRIKADELLER
With Cucumber Salad

Everyone here, or there, has his own way of making meatballs (Frikadeller). The big difference in the Danish variety is the combination of beef, veal and pork very finely ground. Your own meat loaf or meatball recipes will serve as well, and this is a tasty way to wind up the leftovers.

*1 slice pumpernickel bread
Slices (¼- to ½-inch) meatballs or meat loaf
Slices Cucumber Salad,* drained*

Cover bread with meat slices, mounding toward the middle. Radiate slices of cucumber from center top in four rows.

SMORREBROD SHRIMP SALAD

Experts recommend using canned shrimp in this salad, and it's a delicious cinch to make with what's on hand.

1 slice pumpernickel bread   Mayonnaise
Canned tiny shrimp with   Canned asparagus tips
    some liquid   1 slice lemon, cut and twisted

Cover bread with mixture of shrimp, mayonnaise flavored with some shrimp liquid and ½-inch cuts of asparagus. Twist a slice of lemon on top.

CHICKEN BREAST WITH SHRIMP SALAD

An old standby in a new flavor combination.

1 slice pumpernickel bread   Smørrebrød Shrimp Salad*
Chicken breast slices   Mimosa egg garnish
Sliced tomato

Cover bread with slices of chicken. Place a slice of tomato in center. Arrange shrimp salad in a ring around outer edge. Scatter mimosa garnish over tomato.

SYLTE
With Vinegar Beets* and Cress

Homemade pork and veal loaf makes a perfect foil for tangy red beets and tart watercress.

1 slice pumpernickel   Watercress sprig
1 slice Sylte (Sylta*)
Vinegar Beets* or small
    whole canned pickled beets

Cover bread with a generous slice of sylte (Sylta*). Garnish with slices of vinegar beets (pickled beets) and watercress sprig.

DANISH BLUE CHEESE
With Blue Grapes and Carrot

Unusual, "Yes!" But good . . . flavor and color well attuned.

1 slice pumpernickel bread   *Concord grapes, seeded halves*
Danish blue cheese   *Carrot, finely grated*

Spread bread with cheese. Place a few grapes, skin-side up, over cheese. Sprinkle with carrot gratings.

DANISH "CROWDED" SHRIMP

Picture an abundance of tiny shrimp, side by side, tails and shoulders resting in buttered bread . . . and you have one of the best sandwiches imaginable. At Oskar Davidsen's in Copenhagen, customers decide on just how shrimp-y they feel . . . there are four different-sized portions. The smallest includes well over 30 shrimp, there's a "double," running from 80 to 100, and finally a pyramid design done for artistic appetites.

1 slice wheat bread   *1 teaspoon mayonnaise*
1 jar tiny Danish, Iceland   *1 slice lemon, cut and twisted*
  or San Francisco shrimp

Cover bread neatly with as many shrimp as desired. Put a dab of mayonnaise on top. Add an airy lemon twist.

SMOKED SALMON
With Scrambled Egg

The salty salmon is balanced by a bland garnishing of egg and a few asparagus tips; it is freshened with dill.

1 slice pumpernickel or wheat bread
3 thin slices smoked salmon
Scrambled Egg[1]

Canned green asparagus tips, drained
Chopped fresh dill

Cover bread with salmon. Garnish with diagonal stripe of scrambled egg. Place asparagus tips on each side. Sprinkle dill over egg.

DANISH SALAMI OR CERVELAT
With Potato Salad

Probably one of the simplest, cheapest and most satisfactory sandwiches on anybody's list.

1 slice wheat bread
Slices salami or cervelat sausage

Potato salad, mayonnaise type
Chives or green onions

Cover bread with sausage. Pile a mound of potato salad in middle. Sprinkle chopped chives or green onion slices over it.

SANDWICH TIPS

Making and Wrapping Sandwiches

1. Make fillings ahead. Cover and refrigerate. They should be moist, but not squishy or drippy. When making sandwiches with

[1] Scrambled egg is made by adding 1 tablespoon of milk or cream to each beaten egg; stir in a buttered skillet until egg is set, but not dry.

sliced meats, 2 or 3 thin slices meat or cheese are more appealing than one thick slab.

2. When trimming crusts and spreading sandwiches, keep bread and filled sandwiches covered with saran film and a damp towel.

3. Wrap sandwiches for lunches and picnics individually or in packets for each person. Pack dainty tea or cocktail sandwiches in trays or shallow pans. Cover with saran film, then a damp towel. Refrigerate.

4. For portable sandwiches, pack items such as lettuce, tomatoes, cucumber, pickles, etc., separately in saran film or plastic bags.

Freezing Party Sandwiches

1. Spread bread with soft butter or margarine. Mayonnaise tends to separate when frozen.

2. Use fillings such as minced or finely chopped chicken, ham, beef or tuna, crab, shrimp, egg yolk and most cheese, grated. Egg whites tend to toughen in freezing. Tomatoes, radishes, celery and such also suffer in freezing and should be added later.

3. Place closed-type sandwiches in layers in shallow boxes or trays; cover each layer with saran film, then overwrap whole tray with saran film. Stack ribbons, rolls, etc., on trays or in pans and overwrap with saran film or foil.

4. Thaw sandwiches in wrappings 1 to 2 hours before serving. Hold in refrigerator if not served as soon as thawed.

HEARTY SANDWICHES

By any name, in any land, crusty bread filled with meat or fish or cheese and relishes makes a happy meal in hand. Here are a number of popular hearties for alfresco suppers, a picnic by a stream, midnight feasts or any hungry-time at all.

HEROS AND SUBMARINES

It's no wonder kids of all ages love these—they're so much fun to make and eat. Use individual French rolls or the small loaves variously called flutes, batons, submarine rolls or *petit pain.*

Split submarine or hero loaves or regular French rolls and smear with olive oil or butter. Cover bottom half with thin slices provolone, Swiss or Cheddar cheese, sliced green or red sweet pepper and thinly sliced red or white onion. Season with salt and pepper, a sprinkle of oil and vinegar. Cover with slices of salami, bologna, mortadella or other spicy sausage and top with slices of tomato. Season with salt, pepper, oil and vinegar and top with pickled hot peppers or sweet cherry peppers. Add layer of ham slices or other specialty meats and cover with top half of bread. Wrap in saran film and press halves together firmly so all will hang together when you cut it. Serve one apiece or cut large loaves in halves or thirds. Serve with olives and pickles. Good with cold beer or Sangria.*

PAN BAGNA

This "bathed bread" of Provence is no doubt one of the forerunners of our submarines and heros.

Split fresh French rolls or *petit pain* in half lengthwise and rub with cut clove of garlic. Spread with butter, or as they do in Provence smear with olive oil. Cover with a thick layer of black olives, pitted and crisp slices green or red sweet pepper. Sprinkle with olive oil, salt and pepper and cover with sliced tomatoes. Season these, then top with anchovies or sardines and capers. Dash again with a little oil and vinegar or lemon juice. Press halves together, wrap tightly in saran film and put heavy weight on top for about 30 minutes.

PEDA SAN

Cut large flat Armenian or Syrian bread into husky chunks about 3×6 inches each. Split and rub with cut clove of garlic. (Spread with olive oil or butter, if you wish, though in its native land this bread is not.) Cover bottom half with thinly sliced onion; green or red sweet peppers, roasted; sliced tomatoes; seasonings and strips or chunks of Greek feta or Armenian string cheese. Monterey Jack, Muenster or mozzarella cheese gives somewhat the same texture and mild flavor. Cover with top half of bread. Serve with black olives and vinegar peppers.

MEXICAN HERO

Cut French rolls in half and spread lightly with butter. Cover bottom half with husky slices Monterey Jack cheese and top with slices of canned green chiles, seeded and blotted dry. Add layer of finely shredded iceberg lettuce and chopped tomato and onion mixed. Season with salt and pepper (seasoned salt and pepper is nice here) and Mexican hot sauce.† Cover with top of roll. Serve with ice cold Mexican beer and warm refried beans or chile beans.

REUBEN SANDWICH

Originally a prize-winner in a hot sandwich contest, this has become a classic served hot or cold. Some say sauerkraut, others say cole slaw. Use whichever you prefer.

For each sandwich, butter 2 large slices pumpernickel or Russian rye bread. Cover one slice with several thin slices Swiss cheese, several thin slices corned beef spread with a good German mustard. Top with drained cole slaw or sauerkraut and second slice of bread. Serve with more cole slaw, dill pickles and cold beer.

TURF CLUB SPECIAL

The chef's version of a Dagwood.

For each sandwich, toast and butter 3 large slices white or Vienna bread. On bottom slice, put several thin slices baked or boiled ham, top with slices Swiss Emmenthal, lettuce leaves and a bit of mayonnaise. Add second slice of toast. Cover with sliced chicken or turkey, lettuce, mayonnaise, then slices of tomato and crisp bacon. Dress with a little mayonnaise, salt and pepper and a leaf of lettuce. Cover with third slice of toast. Secure with picks and cut sandwich on the diagonal into 3 pieces. Garnish with stuffed olives and pickles. Serve with potato salad.

CRAB LOAF

Split a long French loaf and spread generously with mayonnaise or Louis Dressing.* Top with a pound of chilled fresh crab meat, in big pieces. Either Dungeness crab or Alaska King crab legs are excellent here. Cover with the Louis dressing or mayonnaise thinned with lemon juice and put top in place. Cut into 4 jumbo sandwiches. Serve with lemon wedges, and sliced avocado and tomatoes. And with it all, ice cold beer.

SHRIMP REMOULADE ROLLS

Cut slice off top of French rolls and hollow insides leaving a thick crusty shell. Butter lightly. Toss small cooked or canned shrimp with chopped celery and Sauce Remoulade* to moisten. Heap into rolls.

TUNA CAPER BOATS

Cut slice off top of French or other favorite rolls and hollow insides leaving a thick crusty shell. Combine flaked canned tuna with chopped celery, hard-cooked eggs and enough mayonnaise to moisten well. Heap into rolls.

TEA AND SPECIAL SANDWICHES

These are the daintier kind, made with very thin bread and often rolled or cut in fancy shapes for teas, receptions, cocktail parties and the like. All can be made ahead, wrapped in saran film and chilled. Some may be frozen (see Freezing Party Sandwiches*).

SHRIMP ROLLS

The filling here is made with the shrimp paste or potted shrimp so beloved by the English for their high teas.

32 slices very thin, fresh, white, firm-textured bread
*Shrimp Paste**
Watercress or parsley

Trim crusts from bread and flatten each slice slightly with rolling pin. Spread each with about 1 tablespoon shrimp paste and roll up tightly. Place close together, seam-side down on tray and cover with a damp towel until all are spread. Wrap tray tightly with saran film, top with the damp towel and refrigerate. Before arranging sandwiches on plate, tuck tiny sprig of watercress or parsley in one end of each. Makes 32 sandwich rolls.

Shrimp Paste

Grind or mash with wooden spoon 2 cups drained, freshly cooked small shrimp or 2 cans (4½ ounces each) tiny shrimp, drained and rinsed. Blend in ½ cup soft butter, ¼ cup mayonnaise, dash salt, ½ teaspoon ground mace (vary with finely chopped fresh or dried dill on occasions); a little cayenne pepper. Blend with spoon until very smooth. Makes about 2 cups.

GINGER RIBBONS

1 package (8 ounces) cream
   cheese
1½ teaspoons Maggi
   seasoning†
1 teaspoon grated lemon peel

¼ cup soft butter
⅓ cup finely chopped
   candied ginger
12 slices thin white bread
12 slices thin wheat bread

Soften cheese with Maggi seasoning and blend in rest of filling ingredients. Trim crusts from bread and spread about 1 tablespoon filling on each of 6 slices wheat bread. Top with white slice and spread it. Repeat with wheat, more filling and white bread. Press stacks firmly together, place in tray and cover with saran film. Cover with damp towel and refrigerate. Before serving, place stacks on cutting board. With a serrated bread knife, using a sawing motion, cut each stack into four ½-inch fingers. Cut each finger into 3 ribbons. Arrange on plates. Makes 6 dozen tiny ribbon sandwiches.

CHUTNEY RIBBONS

Substitute ¼ cup finely chopped, drained chutney and 2 tablespoons finely crumbled bacon bits for the candied ginger in recipe above.

PINK RIBBONS

Especially pretty for a girls' tea or a fancy reception. Make ribbon sandwiches following directions for Ginger Ribbons.* Use thin white bread only and Shrimp Paste* for the filling. Tint filling, if necessary, a soft shrimp pink with a few drops red food coloring.

EGG RINGS

1 loaf unsliced white or
   wheat bread
About ¼ cup butter or
   mayonnaise

Cheesy Egg Spread*
Mayonnaise and finely minced
   parsley, optional
Watercress or capers

Cut bread lengthwise in thin slices and cut into rounds with small cooky or biscuit cutter. Spread half the rounds lightly with butter or mayonnaise and top each with spoonful of spread. With small doughnut cutter, cut doughnut holes from rest of rounds; place rings on top of the spread sandwiches. Press gently together. If you like, brush edges lightly with mayonnaise and roll in minced parsley. Arrange on tray, cover with saran film, then a damp towel. Refrigerate. At serving time, decorate each with tiny sprig of watercress or a caper. Makes 30 to 36 small sandwiches.

Cheesy Egg Spread

Mash 6 warm hard-cooked eggs and blend in ⅓ cup grated Cheddar cheese, 3 tablespoons crumbled blue cheese, ½ teaspoon salt, freshly ground pepper and a few drops onion juice, if you wish. Moisten with a little mayonnaise, if necessary. Makes about 2 cups.

Pumpernickel Rounds:

Cut thin slices pumpernickel in small rounds. Add a little garlic salt or puréed garlic to Cheesy Egg Spread.* Heap lightly onto bread. Top each with a caper.

PISTACHIO RINGS

Almonds, filberts or pine nuts also make interesting and delicious fresh nut butters for tea and cocktail sandwiches. This is more exotic and a beautiful green color.

To make pistachio nut butter, place 1½ cups blanched pistachio nuts in electric blender (in three portions). Add a total of 1½ to 2 tablespoons fine salad oil and whizz until smooth. Stop motor often as needed to push nuts into blades. If no blender is available, grind nuts finely several times and blend with oil. Salt to taste. You will have about 1 cup ground nuts. Whip in an equal amount (or double if you wish) of soft butter. Cover and chill. Stir smooth again when ready to use—it separates. Make small sandwiches following directions for Egg Rings* using pistachio butter as filling. Brush edges with mayonnaise and decorate with shredded pistachios for a fancy effect. Pistachio butter also makes pretty ribbon sandwiches.

SMOKED SALMON SQUARES

Spread small thin slices pumpernickel bread with softened cream cheese. Season cheese with a few drops onion juice if you wish. Top with thin slice of smoked salmon, a sprig of fresh dill. Cover with second slice of bread or serve open-face.

HAM IN BRIOCHE

Split brioche (frozen brioche are available and some fancy bakeries often make small party-size brioche) and spread both sides with sweet butter. Fill with several wafer-thin slices of Virginia or country-type smoked ham and sliced breast of roast chicken.

PATE EN BRIOCHE

Split small brioche and butter both sides with sweet butter. Spread or fill with slices of Chicken Liver Appetizer,* Walnut Bourbon Pâté* or New Orleans Shrimp Pâté.*

CHAPTER VIII

Desserts

Desserts are morale builders, the final pleasant ending to a meal. Though the tendency today is to cut down on such, or even eliminate, dinner is disappointing and incomplete without something to soothe the taste buds after sharp salads and savory meats. A dessert need not be sticky sweet or gooey rich—in fact we hope it won't be. Except for parties and special occasions, most of us are content with a cool pear or apple and a slim wedge of cheese, or a pretty bunch of grapes or a dish of bright berries with a cooky. But there comes a time when nothing satisfies but a luscious, hang-it-all-with-calories-and-cholesterol dessert.

This longing for something sweet is dateless and apparently universal. The English love their sweets of puddings and cakes, the French their elegant crèmes and soufflés. Italians delight more in their beautiful fruits and ices except on feast days and special occasions. While the opposite is true in Middle Europe where rich tortes of nuts and chocolate are enjoyed with coffee *mit schlag* from around noon on till late at night. The sweets of the Middle East and India, Mexico and many Latin American countries are truly that and usually much too sweet for the American taste. But they provide good ideas for exciting adaptations.

The baking of fancy cakes and tortes, complicated meringues and intricate fruit pastries, European women leave to the bakers who pride themselves on these specialties. But American women seem to take more pride in their dessert making than in any other type of cooking. They are constantly on the lookout for a new make-ahead concoction for their bridge group, for a special VIP luncheon or an ultra something the boss will remember when he comes to dinner.

The desserts here fill all these needs and many more, where the emphasis is on coolness, convenience and mouth-watering flavor.

Some are simple fruit desserts, but all elegant and beautiful. There are luscious creams and molds, velvety mousses and unusual pies and meringues. And the favorite desserts of everyone, wonderful ice creams and sherbets which appear as themselves or are fashioned into fabulous bombes and frozen pies and tortes. Naturally everything is made ahead, chilled or frozen, and waiting for that hushed, expectant moment when the dessert is brought forth in dulcet splendor.

CELESTIAL STRAWBERRIES

Beautiful berries bathed in a ruby sauce of crushed berries, currant jelly and orange liqueur.

2 pint baskets strawberries
½ cup red currant jelly
2 tablespoons Cointreau or other orange-flavored liqueur
Whipped cream, optional

Rinse, hull and dry berries on paper towels. Put 1 cup in blender, the rest in bowl. Cover and chill bowl. Set jelly and liqueur in small pan over low heat until melted. Pour into blender over strawberries; whizz until smooth. Chill. Shortly before serving, place whole berries in glass serving bowl and pour sauce over them. Mix gently. You may pass a bowl of softly whipped cream separately, but it's really sacrilege. Makes 4 servings.

Note: This lovely sauce is delicious on peaches, pears, nectarines, bananas, melon mixtures, papaya.

ICEBERG BANANAS

An entirely new taste sensation! Frozen bananas sauced with cream and cinnamon-sugar. Made in instants with the cooperation of your freezer.

For each serving, peel a ripe banana and wrap in saran film. Twist ends tightly to exclude air. Place in freezer to freeze solid, 4 hours or more. At serving time, place bananas on cutting board and slice thinly, on the diagonal, with a heavy French knife. Mound in shallow glass bowls and sprinkle lightly with sugar mixed with a dash of cinnamon. Slowly pour heavy cream over bananas coating each slice lightly. Cream freezes almost instantly when it hits the frozen fruit. Hurry dessert to the table.

NECTARINES VANILLE

Poached whole fruit redolent of vanilla bean and a little kirsch.

12 ripe but firm large
  nectarines
1½ cups sugar
2 pieces (2 inches each)
  vanilla bean, split (or 1½
  tablespoons pure vanilla
  extract)

1 tablespoon shredded orange
  peel
3 tablespoons kirsch or brandy
¼ cup lightly toasted almond
  slivers
Sauce Romanoff* or Berry
  Berry Sauce*

Drop nectarines, one at a time, into boiling water for 10 to 20 seconds. Lift out; blanch under cold water and pull off skin with aid of paring knife. Combine sugar, ¾ cup water and vanilla bean (or extract) in large heavy saucepan. Bring to boil; simmer 5 minutes. Poach nectarines 4 or 5 at a time in simmering syrup until just tender and still shapely, 8 to 12 minutes. Do not overcook. Remove with slotted spoon to bowl until all are cooked. Add orange peel and kirsch to syrup and simmer until thickened. Pour over fruit. Chill several hours. At serving time, set nectarines upright in a pyramid in shallow bowl; pour syrup over them. Sprinkle with almonds. Serve desired sauce in separate bowl. Makes 6 servings.

SAUCE ROMANOFF

There are numerous versions of this famous ice-creamy sauce originally made for strawberries. This is ours, which is easy and superb with almost any fruit.

1 *pint vanilla ice cream*
4 *tablespoons kirsch, brandy, Cointreau, rum or whatever*
    flavor best suits the fruit
1 *cup heavy cream, whipped*

Soften ice cream by beating quickly in electric mixer. Quickly beat in kirsch, then fold in whipped cream. Return to freezer a couple of hours before serving. Makes about 3½ cups.

GOLDEN PEARS

Handle pears gently and don't overcook for a truly beautiful effect.

2 *tablespoons slivered orange*   ¾ *cup water*
    peel (peel of 1 orange)   ¾ *cup fresh orange juice*
½ *cup sugar*   6 *perfect, firm-ripe pears*

To make slivered peel, cut thin peel from orange with vegetable peeler. Try to get only the orange part; cut away any white membrane. Cut peel into pin-size slivers with heavy French knife. Cover with water and heat to boiling. Simmer 10 minutes; drain, rinse with cold water and drain. Meanwhile, stir sugar, water and orange juice together in deep saucepan. Heat to boiling then simmer gently 10 minutes. Carefully peel pears keeping them whole and stems intact. Place in hot syrup, 3 at a time if necessary. Add orange slivers. Cook gently about 8 minutes, basting pears and carefully turning with two wooden spoons. Do not overcook. Remove carefully to bowl. Boil syrup a few minutes to thicken; pour over pears. Cool and chill, basting pears now and then. To serve, stand pears upright in shallow crystal bowl and pour syrup over them. Makes 6 servings.

STRAWBERRIES ROMANOFF, CUYAMACA

In San Diego, the Cuyamaca Club serves a good variation of Strawberries Romanoff. It's their traveling maître d's German version.

1 pint vanilla ice cream
⅓ cup cream sherry
1 cup heavy cream, whipped
4 cups (2 baskets) fresh strawberries

⅓ cup (or more) sugar
2 tablespoons kirsch
½ cup Grand Marnier
¼ cup orange curaçao

Follow recipe method for Sauce Romanoff,* but substitute ⅓ cup cream sherry for recommended liqueurs. Clean strawberries, remove stems and sugar berries, according to tartness. Let stand about an hour to let berries absorb sugar. Thirty minutes before serving add mixture of kirsch, Grand Marnier and orange curaçao; chill in covered container. To serve, spoon a little sauce Romanoff into bottom of dessert or parfait glasses; add drained strawberries, but reserve 6 or 8 pretty berries for garnishing. Spoon remaining sauce over berries. Top each serving with a single berry. Makes 6 to 8 servings.

CHERRIES IN PORT

Spiced cherries in a wine-flavored jelly. The ideal dessert after a hearty dinner.

¾ cup sugar
2 cups water
6 whole cloves
1 piece (2 inches) stick cinnamon
1 strip (4 inches) orange or lemon peel
1 cup port wine

3 cups fresh, sweet cherries (Bing), pitted
2 envelopes unflavored gelatine
½ cup orange juice
1 tablespoon brandy, optional
Cream or Almond Custard Sauce*

Combine in medium saucepan the sugar, water, spices and peel. Bring to boil and simmer 5 minutes. Add port and cherries, also a few cherry pits for extra cherry flavor. Simmer 5 minutes longer. Sprinkle gelatine over orange juice and stir into hot mixture. Add brandy if desired. Cover and cool 30 minutes. Scoop out spices and cherry pits with a slotted spoon. Pour gelatine into 5-cup mold or pretty glass bowl; chill several hours, until set. Unmold on chilled plate or rough up the jelly slightly with fork if mixture is chilled in bowl. Serve plain, with cream or chilled almond custard sauce. Makes 6 servings.

HEARTS AND GUAVAS

In the Caribbean guava shells are served over cream cheese, but we think our way is more delicate over molded coeurs à la crème.

2 teaspoons gelatine	1 cup light cream
3 tablespoons cold water	1 tablespoon powdered sugar
1 pint (2 cups) cottage cheese	¼ teaspoon salt
1 package (8 ounces) cream cheese	Guava Shells*

Sprinkle gelatine over cold water in small saucepan. Force cottage cheese through fine sieve into large electric mixer bowl. Add cream cheese, cream, sugar and salt. Beat to blend ingredients. Heat softened gelatine slowly until dissolved. Beat into cheese mixture. Lightly oil 8 to 10 individual heart-shaped molds (depending on size) or one 4-cup heart mold. Fill molds; cover with saran film. Chill 4 hours or more. Unmold on chilled dessert plate. Place guava pieces and syrup on each serving. Makes 8 to 12 servings.

Guava Shells

If you are fortunate enough to have access to fresh guavas:

2 cups guava shells[1]	1 cup water
1 cup sugar	3 slices lemon

[1] If fresh guavas are not available, 2 cans (1 pound, 2 ounces each) guava shells are approximate equivalent. Fresh or frozen, crushed and sweetened strawberries or raspberries will also serve.

Select ripe guavas. Wash, remove stems and blossom ends. Cut guavas in half and remove seeds. Put guava shells in a saucepan with sugar, water and lemon; cook over medium heat 15 to 20 minutes, or until syrup has thickened slightly and guavas are tender. Chill 2 hours. Remove lemon before serving. Serve "shells" as sauce over coeurs. About 3 cups sauce.

CITRON FROMAGE
Lemon Chiffon Pudding

A Scandinavian recipe, which seems to have as many variations as there are Scandinavian women cooking it. We like the tart lemony fluff accented with red raspberry sauce.

1 envelope unflavored gelatine	Juice 2 lemons
¼ cup cold water	Grated peel ½ lemon
4 eggs, separated	Pinch salt
¾ cup sugar	Red Raspberry Sauce*

Sprinkle gelatine over cold water. Beat egg yolks in top part of double boiler; add ⅔ cup sugar and stir to blend. Cook and stir over hot, not boiling water for 10 to 15 minutes, until thickened. Remove from heat. Add softened gelatine and stir to dissolve. Add lemon juice and peel. Cool it. Beat egg whites with salt in a deep bowl until almost stiff. Gradually add remaining sugar, a tablespoonful at a time; continue beating until shiny and stiff. Fold egg whites into lemon mixture. Pile citron fromage into lightly oiled 3- to 4-cup mold or into individual dessert glasses. Refrigerate 4 or more hours before serving. Serve with red raspberry sauce. Makes 5 to 6 servings.

Red Raspberry Sauce

    1 package (10 ounces) frozen red raspberries
    1 tablespoon cornstarch

Defrost berries and drain ½ cup of juice from them. Blend cornstarch into 2 tablespoons of juice in small saucepan. Add remaining juice.

Cook and stir over low heat until thickened, about 5 minutes. Remove from heat; add berries. Check sweetness, you may wish more sugar; if so, add it now. Chill it. Offer it in a sauce server with dessert. Makes 1¼ cups sauce.

LICHEE PINK SNOW

The delicate, unusual flavor belies description, but fits whenever a light dessert is desired. Don't wait for an oriental meal to try this one.

1 can (1 pound, 4 ounces)
    seedless lichee fruit†
1 envelope unflavored gelatine
1 cup boiling water
⅓ cup sugar
⅛ teaspoon salt

2 tablespoons lemon juice
2 tablespoons Hawaiian Punch
    concentrate
1 teaspoon almond extract
1 egg white
Almond Custard Sauce*

Drain and reserve liquid from canned lichee fruit. Pour ½ cup lichee liquid into bowl; sprinkle gelatine over it. Let soften a few minutes. Pour boiling water over to dissolve it. Add sugar and salt; stir to dissolve. Taste remaining lichee liquid to check sweetness; this varies among oriental canneries. If not sweet enough, add 1 to 2 tablespoons more sugar to gelatine mixture. Measure remaining lichee liquid; there should be 1 cup, but this also varies. If liquid is short the amount, add water. Add lichee liquid, lemon juice, Hawaiian Punch and flavoring to gelatine. Chill until syrupy. Beat egg white quite stiff; fold into gelatine with lichee fruit. Pour pink snow into parfait or dessert glasses to chill in refrigerator 4 or more hours. Serve with a sauce boat of almond custard sauce. Makes 4 servings.

Almond Custard Sauce

Follow directions for sauce on egg custard package mix, or make as described below.

3 egg yolks
¼ cup sugar
Pinch salt

2 cups milk
1 teaspoon almond extract

Beat egg yolks lightly in saucepan. Add sugar and a good pinch of salt. Scald milk and stir into egg yolks. Place saucepan over low heat, stirring constantly. Or, the custard may be cooked in upper part of double boiler (gently boiling water in bottom pan should not touch upper pan), with an occasional stirring. Stir until custard starts to thicken and coats spoon. Remove from all heat immediately. (If necessary, set pan in cold water to keep custard from curdling and strain it.) Cool custard; add flavoring. Chill in refrigerator 4 hours or more. Makes over 2 cups of sauce.

MOUSSE AU CHOCOLAT

Easiest of all the chocolate mousses to make and still our favorite.

1 package (6 ounces) semi-sweet chocolate pieces
2 tablespoons sugar
¼ cup orange curaçao
1 teaspoon instant coffee, optional
5 eggs, separated

Combine chocolate, sugar, liqueur and coffee in top of double boiler. Melt over hot (not boiling) water. Stir occasionally, until smooth. Still over hot water with heat off beat in egg yolks, one by one. Cool slightly. Beat egg whites until stiff but not dry; gently fold into chocolate. Pour into small soufflé dishes, French petit pots, demitasse or small teacups. Cover with saran film and chill overnight. Top with Crème Chantilly, if you like—1 cup heavy cream whipped until thick with 1 tablespoon powdered sugar. Stir in 1 tablespoon curaçao. Makes 8 servings.

CREME AU CARAMEL

In Spain and Latin America they say flan, at home we call it caramel custard. The bit of Grand Marnier added by the owner-chef in a side-street Riviera bistro is sheer Gallic genius, we think. The sweet caramel sauce literally sings.

½ cup sugar for caramel
3 cups milk
6 tablespoons sugar for custard
3 whole eggs
3 egg yolks

Dash salt
1 teaspoon vanilla
1 to 2 tablespoons Grand Marnier or other orange-flavored liqueur

Have ready a 1-quart mold or casserole (metal preferred). In heavy skillet, place ½ cup sugar and cook without stirring, shaking pan occasionally, until it forms a light golden caramel syrup. Stir to blend, then quickly pour into mold, turning mold round and round until syrup coats bottom and sides completely, and syrup stops running. Turn mold upside down and set aside. Scald milk only until bubbles appear around edges. With whisk, gradually beat sugar into eggs and yolks until mixture is blended, light and foamy. Gradually pour in hot milk, beating constantly with whisk. Add salt and vanilla. Strain into mold. Set in pan containing hot water to one-half the depth of mold. Cook at 325 degrees F. 50 to 60 minutes, or until a silver knife thrust in the center is clean when removed. Custard is still a little shaky in center. Remove from heat and cool. Refrigerate overnight. Loosen around edges with tip of small spatula, then invert over shallow dish. Shake gently until custard is free of mold. If some of caramel clings to mold, add a little hot water or Grand Marnier and heat until melted; cool slightly and pour over custard. Just before serving, pour a tablespoon Grand Marnier over custard. Makes 6 servings.

ICED STRAWBERRY SOUFFLE

Actually the iced soufflé is a fluffy Bavarian cream chilled in a soufflé dish with an extended collar tied around it. Perfect make-ahead for a dressy dinner.

2 pint baskets strawberries	1 tablespoon lemon juice,
2 envelopes unflavored gelatine	or to taste
1 cup sugar	Dash salt
6 eggs, separated	1 cup heavy cream

To prepare soufflé dish: lightly oil a triple-fold strip of heavy foil. Tie it around 1½-quart soufflé dish or other straight-sided casserole making a collar that extends 2 inches above rim of dish. Secure ends with cellophane tape.

Set aside 1 cup of strawberries for garnish. Wash and hull rest; purée in blender or force through strainer. You should have 1½ cups. Mix gelatine with ½ cup sugar in top of double boiler or heavy saucepan. Stir in egg yolks with whisk, then add ¾ cup strawberry purée. Cook over hot water or very low heat stirring constantly until sauce thickens slightly into a soft custard. Remove from heat and blend in lemon juice. Chill, stirring now and then until mixture is cool. Add rest of purée and chill until it will mound softly. Beat egg whites with salt until soft peaks form. Gradually beat in remaining ½ cup sugar until meringue is shiny and holds definite peaks. Whip cream until it holds shape, then pile on top of egg whites. Spoon a little of this into thick strawberry purée, then gently fold purée into meringue mixture. Spoon gently into prepared dish. Chill 6 hours or overnight. Carefully remove collar. Decorate top with halved strawberries. Makes 8 servings.

ANGELA PIA

With this title Pietro's in San Francisco must be kidding! A Pious
Angel . . . with liquor? No matter, it's a fluff of delectable stuff
and just great after a heavy dinner.

3 eggs, separated
½ cup sugar
2 tablespoons brandy
2 tablespoons rum

½ pint (1 cup) heavy cream
1 teaspoon vanilla
1 envelope unflavored gelatine
¼ cup cold water

In a large electric mixer bowl beat egg yolks until thick and light;
add sugar gradually. Continue beating until very creamy, blending
in brandy and rum. Beat egg whites until stiff, but not dry. Whip
cream until stiff enough to peak; add vanilla. Sprinkle gelatine over
water in saucepan; when softened, gradually heat it until gelatine
dissolves. Blend gelatine into egg yolks. Fold egg whites and
whipped cream into egg yolks. Pour into cocktail or parfait glasses.
Chill 2 hours or more before serving. Makes 6 to 8 servings.

RICE IMPERIAL

Our shortcut way with a classic.

½ cup long grain rice
2½ cups milk
1 piece (2 inches) stick
   cinnamon
1 tablespoon shredded orange
   peel
½ cup sugar
1 envelope unflavored
   gelatine

1 teaspoon vanilla
1 cup heavy cream, whipped
1 can (1 pound, 13 ounces)
   cling peach halves
½ cup orange or ginger
   marmalade
1 tablespoon lemon juice
1 tablespoon cream sherry

Combine rice, 1½ cups milk, cinnamon and orange peel in heavy
saucepan. Cover tightly and simmer gently until very tender and
liquid is absorbed, about 30 to 45 minutes. Remove cinnamon. Com-

bine sugar, gelatine and remaining cup of milk in small saucepan; stir over low heat until gelatine melts. Add vanilla and blend into rice. Chill until thickened, but not set. Fold in whipped cream and pack in lightly oiled 5-cup fluted mold. Chill 3 to 4 hours. Combine ½ cup syrup from peaches with marmalade; simmer 5 minutes. Add peaches and heat just to boiling. Add lemon juice and sherry. Cool and chill. Unmold rice on serving plate and stand peaches around base of mold. Pour sauce over mold and peaches. Makes 8 servings.

FRESH RASPBERRY ICE CREAM

So creamy and fruity-crunchy, this seasonal dessert is a regular Crosby family project. After all, is there anything that tastes better or is more fun making than good old-fashioned ice cream?

2 pints fresh raspberries	2 teaspoons vanilla
1½ cups sugar	2 cups heavy cream
1 cup milk	Crushed ice
Pinch salt	Rock salt
2 egg yolks	

Wash, pick over and drain raspberries; empty in bowl. Sprinkle with ¾ cup sugar. Set aside, but stir through occasionally. Scald milk; stir in ¾ cup sugar and salt, until dissolved. Pour milk slowly over beaten egg yolks. Beat to blend with a wire whisk; return mixture to saucepan. Cook custard over low heat until smooth and of a cream consistency. Do not boil. Remove from heat; add vanilla. Chill custard. Add cream. Fill freezer can (about three-quarters full) with ice cream mixture. Insert dasher and attach cover. Set freezer can on bucket bottom knob. Secure bucket-hand crank attachment; test turning it. Pack bucket, in alternate layers, with 1 cup rock salt to every 6 cups crushed ice. Place bucket where it will be easy to turn. Put a pan or bowl under side drip spout to catch draining salt water. Start cranking. Turn crank until it becomes stiff. Remove lids; remove dasher, but do not lift can out. Fold raspberries in and press ice cream down. Replace cover and close opening. Drain off excess water and repack bucket with ice and salt. Let ice cream harden. Makes 2 quarts.

FIRST LADY PAPAYA ICE CREAM

A fragrantly delicous ice cream given us by gracious Beatrice Burns, wife of Governor John A. Burns of Hawaii. Puréed apricots, peaches, bright berries may replace the papaya.

2 ripe Hawaiian papayas
½ cup sugar
2½ tablespoons fresh lemon
  juice

1 cup heavy cream

Halve papayas, scrape out seeds and peel and dice fruit. Force through sieve or food mill (or whizz in blender about 30 seconds). You should have about 1½ cups purée. Mix with sugar, lemon juice and cream. Pour into ice cube tray and freeze quickly with temperature control turned to coldest setting. Stir mixture twice during freezing. When firm, reduce temperature control to normal setting and allow ice cream to "ripen" an hour or so. Makes 1½ pints.

MELON ICE

Coolest thing going—a melon ice served in chilled melon halves.

1 cup sugar
2 cups water
2 teaspoons unflavored gelatine
2 tablespoons cold water
2 tablespoons fresh lemon
  juice
Grated peel 2 limes

3 tablespoons fresh lime juice
1 tablespoon white crème de
  menthe
4 cantaloupes
2 egg whites
Fresh mint leaves or lime
  twists

Bring sugar and 2 cups water to boiling; simmer 5 minutes. Sprinkle gelatine over 2 tablespoons cold water to soften, then stir into hot syrup. Cool slightly and add lemon juice, lime peel and juice, crème de menthe. Pare one cantaloupe, dice the meat and force through food mill or sieve (you should have 1 cup melon purée). Blend into cool syrup and pour into 2 ice cube trays (or a double one) and freeze until mushy. Turn into chilled mixer bowl; add unbeaten egg whites. Beat until light and fluffy. Return to freezer and freeze until firm, 4 to 6 hours. Cut remaining cantaloupes in halves and scrape out seeds. Set each half on chilled dessert plate or in shallow, stemmed coupe glass lined with chipped ice. Fill with melon ice. Decorate with fresh mint or a twist of lime. Makes 6 servings.

FRESH LEMON ICE

Patterned after the delightful fresh fruit ices Italians make so beautifully. Simply puréed fruit or juice sweetened and frozen. Americans usually prefer a smoother texture than the typical snowy ices of Italy, so we've added a little gelatine. Puréed berries, apricots, oranges, melons, etc., may be used. Adjust sugar accordingly.

Italians often freeze their ices in the shell of the fruit—lemon ice in lemon shells, orange in orange shells, pineapple and papaya ice in small pineapple or papaya half-shells. Banked in a bed of chipped ice, an assortment makes a magnificent display for a fancy buffet.

1 cup sugar	¾ cup fresh lemon purée
2 cups water	(about 4 lemons)
2 teaspoons unflavored gelatine, optional	

Stir sugar and water together in saucepan; heat to boiling and boil 5 minutes. Remove from heat. If gelatine is used; sprinkle it over 2 tablespoons cold water to soften. Stir into hot syrup. Chill until cold. To make purée, peel lemons cutting away all white membrane (or use pulp scooped from lemons if you freeze ice in lemon shells). Cut into eighths and cut out white core and remove seeds. Whizz in blender until puréed. Pour through coarse strainer to get out any white bits you missed. Mix with cold syrup. Pour into refrigerator trays and freeze until mushy. In cold bowl with cold beaters, beat with electric mixer until frosty white and fluffy. Return quickly to refrigerator trays and freeze 3 to 4 hours. Should be served softish like old-fashioned homemade ice cream. Makes 1½ pints.

Lemon Cream Sherbet:

Use 1½ cups water for sugar syrup in Fresh Lemon Ice.* When ice is frozen to a mush, beat in 1 unbeaten egg white and ½ cup heavy cream. Freeze.

Lemon Ice in Lemon Shells:

After Fresh Lemon Ice* is beaten, freeze until it is moundable. Heap into large, scooped-out lemon shells (use a grapefruit spoon). Freeze overnight. Remove from freezer 10 to 15 minutes before serving. Serve in coupe glasses lined with chipped ice or on a star of shiny galax leaves.†

Sherbet Stuffed Oranges:

Heap large, scooped-out orange shells with commercial or homemade orange sherbet (follow recipe for Lemon Cream Sherbet,* substituting 1 cup orange juice for lemon purée); freeze. Dash with orange-flavored liqueur at serving time, if you wish.

SPOOM AU CHAMPAGNE

Spoom is fun to sound, but it's not a newly coined word. This dessert, old as sherbet, has been revived from ancient French recipes to spark the menu at the superb Mauna Kea Hotel in Hawaii. There it's served in the traditional manner, with or between main courses, but it also makes a magnificent dessert following a heavy meal.

1 cup sugar
½ teaspoon cream of tartar
½ cup water
4 egg whites

1 pint lemon or pineapple sherbet
Champagne or Rhine wine, Chablis, sauterne or moselle

Add sugar and cream of tartar to water in saucepan; stir and bring to boil. Do not stir while mixture is forming syrup. Cook with candy thermometer until syrup spins a thread, 240 degrees. Remove

Plate No. 4—Airy and luscious *Orange Trifle* (p. 186) is fragrant with fresh orange and capped with a cloud of whipped cream. Photograph courtesy of Sunkist Growers, Inc.

from heat. Beat egg whites very stiffly using a rotary or electric beater. Pour syrup slowly, in a steady stream, over egg whites, and continue to beat until meringue is cool. It should be very thick. Stir sherbet to soften it; then beat sherbet into the Italian meringue on low speed, and for a short time. Fill champagne glasses, or other glasses (which can be placed in freezer) with the spoom. Lace each glass with your favorite champagne, or other light white wine just before serving. Makes about 8 servings.

MOUSSE GRAND MARNIER

A mousse is one of the easiest and most satisfactory of frozen desserts since it freezes smooth and creamy without stirring. Traditionally, it is frozen in a fancy mold and served with a colorful sauce.

2 egg whites	1 cup heavy cream
Salt	¼ cup Grand Marnier
6 tablespoons sugar	Berry Berry Sauce*

Beat egg whites with salt until softly peaked. Gradually beat in ¼ cup sugar until eggs are stiff and shiny. With same beater, whip cream until stiff; beat in rest of sugar. Gently blend in Grand Marnier. Fold in egg whites. Turn mixture into a 1-quart mold or several individual molds. Freeze until firm, 4 hours or overnight. Unmold on serving plate and serve with sauce. Makes 6 to 8 servings.

Berry Berry Sauce:

Richly perfumed and a brilliant color.

Defrost 1 package each (10-ounce size) frozen strawberries and raspberries just enough to drain excess juices. Whizz fruit in blender until smooth. Strain and add Grand Marnier or other orange-flavored liqueur to taste. Makes about 2 cups.

FRANGO

Getting this recipe was a "magnificent obsession" . . . and worth it!

½ cup vanilla wafer crumbs
½ cup butter or ¼ cup
    butter and ¼ cup
    margarine
1 cup powdered sugar, sifted
2 eggs
2 squares (melted) or 2
    packets (redi-blend)
    unsweetened chocolate

½ teaspoon peppermint
    flavoring
1 teaspoon vanilla
Whipped cream
Maraschino cherries, green
    or red

Crush wafers with rolling pin or more easily in a blender. Press ¼ cup crumbs into bottoms of 8 aluminum foil baking cups; reserve other ¼ cup for topping. With electric mixer cream butter in a small deep bowl. Add sugar and beat until fluffy. Add eggs; beat again until light and well mixed. Add melted and cooled chocolate or ready-pourable packets, flavorings and beat thoroughly. Spoon frango into each container; spread evenly. Top with a sprinkling of remaining crumbs. Freeze 2 hours or more. Remove from containers to serve; top with a dab of lightly sweetened whipped cream and a cherry. Makes 8 servings.

RUTH BATEMAN'S CAFE JAMAICA[2]

The most popular dessert at our house for gatherings small and large—served in the living room in our best china cups. It's a makeup from a memorable dessert enjoyed years ago at Chalet Suisse in Mexico City. Recently we ordered it there again and asked the chef exactly what was in his heady concoction. "Just coffee ice cream and dark rum," he answered.

 1 quart best quality, hand-packed coffee ice cream (the airy, fluffy
     kind will melt)
 6 tablespoons dark Jamaica rum (Myers's, or Lemon Hart)
 Whipped cream, optional

With electric mixer, whip slightly softened ice cream and rum together, adding rum by spoonfuls. Don't allow cream to liquify. Return mixture to freezer to firm up somewhat, but it should be served softish so you half-eat and half-drink it. If you wish, just before serving, swirl in a little whipped cream. Spoon into cups. Makes 4 to 5 servings.

ORANGE DIVINE

Another softie ice cream dessert you serve in glasses or cups. Elegant but very easy.

 1 quart vanilla ice cream
 1 can (6 ounces) frozen orange juice concentrate
 ¼ cup Grand Marnier

Spoon ice cream, concentrate in chunks, and liqueur into blender container. Let stand a few minutes to soften slightly. Whizz until smoothly blended but not melted. Pour into cups or glasses and serve at once. Or return to freezer to firm up. Allow to soften before serving. Makes 4 to 5 servings. Try it with strawberry ice cream. Another sensation.

[2] From the I Love to Cook Book by Ruth Conrad Bateman, published by The Ward Ritchie Press, Copyrighted © 1962 by Ruth Conrad Bateman.

PAPAYAS JUBILEE

This dessert sauce is a sunny Hawaiian interpretation of a flameless cherries jubilee—and just about the best cover-up vanilla ice cream ever had.

1 tablespoon cornstarch
1 cup orange juice
1½ teaspoons lime juice
½ cup sugar
Few grains salt
1½ teaspoons finely grated
  orange peel

2 peeled, seeded and cubed
  (3 cups) papayas
Ice cream
Shredded or flaked coconut

Blend cornstarch into ¼ cup orange juice in a saucepan. Add remaining orange juice, lime juice, sugar and salt. Bring to a boil over medium heat, stirring constantly. When thickened and clear, remove it. Add orange peel and papaya. Cool it. Refrigerate 2 to 4 hours. Serve as a dessert sauce over vanilla ice cream. Sprinkle each serving with coconut. Makes 6 to 8 servings.

BOMBE SPECTACULAR

Bombes make dramatic desserts and there's no end to the exciting combinations in colors and flavors you can work out using your own or commercial ice creams, sherbets and mousses. Follow the dozens of classic suggestions given in *The Escoffier Cook Book and Guide to the Fine Art of Cookery*, or make up some of your own.

Use a metal bombe or melon mold—or a metal bowl will do. Chill the mold and freeze contents between layers or additions. A freezer that maintains 0 degrees F. is preferred. Fresh fruits, a pretty sauce richly perfumed with a complementary liqueur or rosettes of whipped cream often decorate the bombes.

1 pint pistachio ice cream
2 tablespoons crème de cassis
  or Grand Marnier
1 pint raspberry or strawberry
  sherbet

Glazed Strawberries* or Berry
  Berry Sauce*

Chill 1-quart melon or other dome-shaped metal mold or bowl. Soften ice cream slightly and use a spoon to press it in an even layer to line the mold. Set in freezer until firm again, at least 30 minutes. With spoon quickly work liqueur into sherbet and fill center of mold. Cover with foil or the metal lid of mold. Freeze until firm, 4 hours or more. To serve, dip mold in very warm water for a few seconds and invert over chilled plate. Shake mold to release bombe. If mold clings, cover with hot, wet towel until bombe frees itself. Return to freezer until serving time. Circle with glazed strawberries or serve berry berry sauce in separate bowl. Makes 6 servings. Double amounts for a large 2-quart, party-size mold.

Glazed Strawberries—Melt ½ cup thin-type apricot jam with 2 tablespoons Grand Marnier or orange juice. Strain. Dip large washed and dried unhulled strawberries in jam. Drain, stem-end down, on wire cake rack placed over sheet of foil.

BOMBE MELBA

Line mold with 1 pint peach ice cream; freeze 30 minutes. Fill with *Raspberry Mousse:* Fold 1 cup sweetened fresh raspberries (or 10-ounce package slightly thawed and drained frozen raspberries) into ¾ cup heavy cream, whipped with 2 tablespoons sugar. Freeze 4 hours or more. Unmold and serve with *Melba Sauce:* Purée in blender 2 packages (10 ounces each) frozen, slightly thawed raspberries with 2 tablespoons red currant jelly. Strain.

BOMBE MARDI GRAS

Line mold with 1 pint butter pecan ice cream; freeze 30 minutes. Fold ¼ cup each drained whole maraschino cherries and semi-sweet chocolate pieces into 1 pint cherry or coffee ice cream. Fill center of mold and freeze 4 hours or more. Unmold and serve with chocolate sauce (there are several excellent dark chocolate sauces or toppings available in cans or jars in supermarkets and specialty shops).

TORTONI RIBBON CAKE

A layered freezer dessert of strawberry ice cream, lemon sherbet and tortoni served with a scarlet strawberry sauce.

2 dozen lady fingers, split and lightly toasted	1 cup heavy cream
	3 tablespoons powdered sugar
1 quart strawberry ice cream	1 teaspoon vanilla
2 tablespoons Cointreau (or orange juice)	1 cup fine, dry macaroon crumbs
1 quart lemon sherbet	Strawberry Sauce*

Line bottom of 8-inch spring form pan with split lady fingers cutting small wedges to fill in all spaces. Stand more lady fingers upright very close together around sides of pan. Soften ice cream slightly with Cointreau; spread evenly over lady finger layer. Top with layer of lady fingers and set in freezer about 30 minutes. Soften sherbet slightly; spread evenly over lady finger layer; return to freezer. Whip cream and powdered sugar together until thick and fluffy; stir in vanilla and fold in crumbs. Swirl over lemon sherbet and cover with saran film. Freeze overnight. About 1 hour before serving make strawberry sauce. Fifteen minutes before serving, remove cake from freezer and release collar on spring form pan. Set cake on serving plate. To serve, cut in small wedges and top each serving with a spoonful of sauce. Makes 12 to 16 servings.

Strawberry Sauce

Wash, dry on paper towels and hull 2 baskets strawberries. Cut larger berries in half, leave rest whole. Sprinkle with a little sugar and 2 tablespoons Cointreau. Cover with saran film and chill 1 hour. Makes about 3 cups.

FROZEN PINEAPPLE PUFFS

The kind of dish young people love to make for their own parties. Tiny cream puffs, pineapple and marshmallows frozen together with ice cream in an angel food pan.

40 tiny Cream Puff Shells*	1 quart vanilla ice cream
1 can (1 pound, 4½ ounces) crushed pineapple	Whipped cream Nuts or maraschino cherries,
2 cups miniature marshmallows	optional

Make and cool cream puff shells. (Several girls can join in this activity.) Combine pineapple and marshmallows. Heat until marshmallows melt, stirring now and then. Chill until ready to use. Arrange half of cream puff shells in bottom of 8-inch tube pan with removable bottom. Spoon half of ice cream over puffs, top with half of sauce. Cover with remaining ice cream. Put rest of cream puffs on top and spoon sauce between puffs. Wrap pan in heavy foil. Freeze 4 to 5 hours or overnight. Just before serving remove from pan and garnish top with swirls of whipped cream (from a pressurized can) and nuts or maraschino cherries if desired. Makes 8 servings.

Cream Puff Shells

Heat ¼ cup butter, ½ cup water and ¼ teaspoon salt to boiling. Add ½ cup sifted flour. Stir vigorously until mixture forms a ball and leaves sides of pan. Remove from heat. Add 2 eggs, one at a time, beating after each addition until smooth and velvety. Drop by scant teaspoonfuls on ungreased baking sheet. Bake in preheated oven (400 degrees F.) about 20 minutes until puffed, dry and golden brown. Cool. Makes 40 puffs.

ORANGE TRIFLE

A fooler, this looks rich and difficult to make, and isn't. It seems mysteriously flavored, and isn't. Delicate sponge cake layers literally soaked in an unusual fresh orange marinade, then topped with soft clouds of whipped cream.

6 eggs	1 teaspoon baking powder
1 cup sugar	Orange Marinade*
3 tablespoons cold water	Whipped Cream Frosting*
½ teaspoon vanilla	1½ cups fresh orange
1 cup sifted cake flour	sections, well drained

Separate eggs, placing 4 whites in small bowl of electric mixer, all yolks in large mixer bowl and reserving 2 whites for use in marinade. Beat yolks until light; gradually add sugar, beating until fluffy and the color of cream. Blend in water and vanilla. Sift together flour and baking powder; gently fold and blend into yolks. Beat the 4 egg whites until stiff, but not dry; carefully fold into batter. Pour equal portions into two greased and floured 9-inch round layer cake pans. Bake at 350 degree F. 30 to 35 minutes, or until tops spring back when lightly touched in center. Allow to cool completely in pans on wire racks; loosen and remove with aid of small spatula. Place one layer top-side down in a flat-bottom, deepish serving bowl. Slowly pour half of orange marinade over it. Top with second layer and evenly pour rest of marinade over it; baste a few seconds. Cover loosely with saran film; refrigerate overnight. Just before serving, swirl clouds of whipped cream frosting over top (sides too if you like); decorate with orange sections. Makes 12 to 16 servings.

Orange Marinade:

2 egg whites (reserved from cake above)	Freshly grated peel 2 oranges (about 2 tablespoons)
¾ cup sugar	
2½ cups fresh orange juice (about 6 large oranges)	

Beat egg whites until soft peaks form; gradually beat in sugar until sharply peaked. Gently stir in orange juice and peel.

Whipped Cream Frosting:

1 cup heavy cream
3 tablespoons powdered sugar
1 teaspoon vanilla

Whip cream until thick and softly peaked. Gradually beat in sugar and vanilla.

VIENNESE MERINGUE TORTE

Tender nutted meringue layers filled and topped with a luscious chocolate cream.

½ cup filberts or blanched
  almonds
4 egg whites, at room
  temperature
Dash salt
½ teaspoon vinegar
1 cup sugar
¾ cup semi-sweet chocolate
  pieces

3 tablespoons hot water
1 teaspoon vanilla
½ teaspoon powdered coffee
1 tablespoon dark rum
1 cup heavy cream
Whipped Cream Rosettes,*
  optional

Spread nuts on cooky sheet and toast at 300 degrees F. about 15 minutes, or until skins can be flaked off filberts or almonds are light gold. Cool and whizz in blender until finely chopped and powdery looking. Beat egg whites with salt and vinegar until soft peaks form. Beat in sugar gradually, beating until meringue stands in very stiff sharp peaks and has a satiny look (takes 10 to 15 minutes). Line 2 cooky sheets with heavy brown paper and mark 2 (8-inch) rounds with cake pan as pattern. Spread meringue on rounds mounding it slightly at sides. Bake in slow oven (275 degrees F.) until dry, 50 to 60 minutes. With small spatula, loosen from paper and carefully remove to wire cake racks. Cool.

Combine chocolate and hot water in top of double boiler. Melt over hot water and blend in vanilla, coffee and rum. Cool until slightly warm, but still liquid. Whip cream until stiff and pour warm chocolate over it in fine stream folding in as you pour. (If chocolate becomes too cold, it will separate in flakes rather than blend into cream. Warm again slightly, or add a few drops hot water to chocolate.) Cream should be smooth, and a light milk chocolate color. Place one meringue on cake plate and spread with half the chocolate. Top with second meringue and rest of chocolate leaving a rim of meringue uncovered. Refrigerate several hours or overnight. Cut torte into small wedges using a sharp, wet knife. Makes 12 servings.

Whipped Cream Rosettes:

If you wish, whip an additional ½ cup heavy cream with a tablespoon powdered sugar. Using a pastry bag with star tube force cream into rosettes over chocolate.

ANGEL PIE, COUNTRY SQUIRE

From Rancho Santa Fe in sunny California, a light and bright meringue with a tart lemony layer . . . this angel pie is about as subtle as a siren's wink!

4 eggs, separated	*Few drops vanilla*
¼ teaspoon cream of tartar	*½ pint (1 cup) heavy cream,*
Pinch salt	* whipped*
1 cup sugar	*Lemon Layer**

Preheat oven to 250 degrees F. Cut a circular piece of brown paper to fit a 9-inch pie pan. Grease it thoroughly; fold and crease it around sides to make it fit contour of pan. Or, if preferred, butter and flour the pan. Beat egg whites with cream of tartar and salt until stiff in large electric mixer bowl. (Reserve egg yolks for lemon layer.) Whites should form big, fat clouds. Add sugar by the tablespoonful, continuously beating. Add vanilla and blend in; do not overbeat. If using brown paper, run it under cold water; the wet paper helps keep meringues from sticking. Pile meringue into pie pan; spread it evenly across top with spatula. Bake in lower half of oven for 20 minutes at 250 degrees F., then 40 minutes at 275 degrees F. Let meringue cool in pan on cake rack. When cool, remove and invert meringue on serving platter. With spatula, spread a thin layer of whipped cream over top and sides. Spread lemon layer over this. Cover whole pie with whipped cream. Chill in refrigerator 4 hours or more. Makes 6 servings.

Lemon Layer:

4 egg yolks
½ cup sugar

Juice 2 lemons
Grated peel of 1 lemon

Put egg yolks in top of double boiler; beat until thick and light. Add sugar, lemon juice and peel. Cook mixture over gently boiling water (not touching bottom of upper pan). Cook and stir until thick. Cool it.

MINIATURE CHEESE CAKES

Despite their wee size, they make an enormous impression. Count on "seconds."

1 package (3 ounces) cream
  cheese, softened
¼ pound (½ cup) butter or
  margarine, softened
1 cup flour

Cheese Filling*
Sour cream, raspberry or
  cherry jam or drained
  crushed pineapple, according
  to preference for topping

Combine cheese, butter and flour; blend to smoothness. Make 12 equal pinch-offs from the dough. Set out 12 foil baking cups in muffin tins. Pat each piece of dough flat and place in bottom of foil cup. Using fingers, shape dough to stretch to lip of cup, pressing against bottom and sides evenly. Spoon filling into each cup. Bake 20 to 25 minutes in preheated 350 degree F. oven. Cool cakes on rack in muffin tins. Remove cakes in their foil containers and chill in refrigerator 4 hours or more. (These cakes may be frozen. Thaw completely before serving.) Spread a teaspoonful of whichever topping you may like on each cake and remove foil cups. Makes 12 servings.

Cheese Filling:

2 packages (3 ounces each)   1 egg
   cream cheese, softened   1 teaspoon vanilla
2 tablespoons sugar

Beat ingredients together and spoon into each cake shell.

CREPES AU FROMAGE

French "big city" dessert crepes are dressed in fancy sauces . . . this is a "country cousin," stuffed with the airiest of cheese fillings.

⅔ cup flour   3 eggs, lightly beaten
½ teaspoon salt   ½ cup milk
1 tablespoon powdered sugar   ¼ cup water
½ teaspoon grated lemon   Fromage Filling*
   peel

Sift dry ingredients into bowl. Add lemon peel. Make a well; pour eggs, milk and water into it. Whisk them together until well blended; don't worry about lumps. You may let batter stand 2 hours; it improves results. Heat 6-inch skillet or crepe pan. Grease it lightly with shortening and a smidgen of butter. Add about 2 tablespoons of batter; tilt pan to spread it around to edges. Cook over medium heat. Watch carefully; when lightly browned on one side, turn it over. Always regrease pan for each pancake. As they are done, stack one on top of the other; or fold over twice, like a lady's handkerchief. Cover and set aside until ready to fill. Makes 12 or more 6-inch crepes.

Fromage Filling:

1 package (8 ounces) cream   1½ tablespoons brandy
   cheese, softened   ½ pint (1 cup) heavy cream
½ pint (1 cup) cottage cheese   1 teaspoon cinnamon
⅓ cup powdered sugar   3 tablespoons sugar
2 teaspoons grated lemon peel

Combine cheeses, sugar, lemon peel and brandy in large electric mixer bowl; beat to blend thoroughly. Whip cream in small, deep bowl; fold into cheese mixture. Put a generous tablespoonful on each crepe; roll it. Place crepes side by side on suitable serving platter or earthenware dish. Spread surplus cheese mixture across top of single- or double-layered crepes, as you would a sauce, such as Hollandaise. Sprinkle with mixture of cinnamon and sugar. Makes about 12 filled crepes or 6 servings.

CHAPTER IX

Drinks ∽

All of us at some time or other are called upon to make cold drinks for a crowd. Maybe tea, iced and spiced for a real warm weather tea party. Or a jugful of lemonade for beach-going chicken and potato salad. Or it could be an icy bowl of sparkling champagne awash with giant strawberries for a particularly important announcement. We've collected a number of special recipes for just such occasions.

'Tis a pity punch has come to be associated with the sweet, insipid brews sometimes served at women's gatherings. Husbands have their own names for such. But punches and coolers can be interesting and exciting whether they're made with spirits or are the nonalcoholic kind that start perhaps with frozen limeade or colorful cranberry juice. The May bowles or light mixtures of young wines and fruits are cooling and pretty. And nothing's more refreshing on a summer day than a frosty pitcher of Spain's Sangria with its fragrance of oranges and lemons and dry red wine.

The secret of all the cold drinks, we feel, is keep them dry or very light on sugar. Oversweetened, they have no refreshment value at all. And serve cold drinks chillingly cold over lots of ice. The tinkle and sparkle of ice is almost as cooling as the touch. Remember too, in making your mixtures, ice will dilute the flavors. So chill juices and wines first, and when appropriate, use flavored ice cubes or even blocks of ice made with juices and the like to cut down on dilution and keep the flavors high. Directions and tips for flavored and decorated ice cubes, ice rings and other garnishes for party drinks are given.

WHIZZER COOLERS

Much of the "shake" has been taken out of home beverage-making. Now, if you're lucky, a little on-off button makes a whizz of this chore. Endless combinations and varieties of icy drinks are smooth and simple in an electric blender. Start your own collection with the following coffee, tea or milk bases; add ice cream or sherbet. Whizz; and moments later, drink deeply with or without a straw. *Relax . . .* it's easy.

MOCHA POLKA

Frosted coffee and chocolate with a zip.

2 *cups (16 ounces) strong,*
  prepared, cool coffee or:
  2 *tablespoons instant coffee*
  plus 1 pint cold water
1 *pint chocolate ice cream*
1 *tablespoon rum or ¼*
  teaspoon almond extract

Pinch salt
Whipped cream
Ground nutmeg or sweet
  chocolate gratings

Put coffee or instant coffee and cold water in blender. Add ice cream, flavoring and salt. Whizz it. Top each glass with a dab of prepared whipped cream and a sprinkling of nutmeg or grated chocolate. Serve at once. Makes four 8-ounce servings.

LEMON-LIME-TIME

More festive than plain tea or lemonade.

2 *cups cold water*
1½ *tablespoons instant tea*
1 *pint lemon or lime sherbet*

1 *bottle or can (about*
  12 *ounces) lemon-lime*
  carbonated beverage

Put water, tea and sherbet in blender. Whizz it. Pour equally into 4 tall glasses. Fill with carbonated beverage. Stir lightly. Serve at once. Makes four 10-ounce servings.

MANGO (OR PEACH) TANGO

An ambrosial whip for midsummer doldrums.

½ to 1 cup milk
2 cups peeled and diced
  mangos or peaches
2 to 3 tablespoons honey,
  optional

3 drops almond flavoring,
  optional
1 pint vanilla ice cream

According to thickness of shake desired, put ½ to 1 cup of milk in blender. Add fruit. If using peaches add 2 to 3 tablespoons honey, according to tartness of fruit, and almond flavoring if desired. Add ice cream; whizz it. Serve at once or chill for later use. Makes about four 10-ounce servings.

ICED EGGNOG

A cool, cool liquid lunch.

1 cup cold milk
2 eggs
1 tablespoon sugar or honey
½ teaspoon vanilla extract

Pinch salt
⅓ cup (about 2 ice cubes)
  crushed ice
Ground nutmeg

Put all ingredients except nutmeg in blender. Whizz it. Pour into 14-ounce glass; sprinkle with nutmeg. Serve at once. Makes a single serving.

YOGURT EAST

Sheminah is the drink that keeps half of Baghdad alive through 120 degree F. summers. As with olives, you may have to drink several samples before you become a follower, but then it's magnetic!

1 cup (1 carton) plain yogurt   1 cup crushed ice
1 cup water   Salt to taste

Put all ingredients in blender. Whizz it. Serve at once. Makes three 8-ounce servings.

YOGURT WEST

Sheminah, with added attractions.

1 cup (1 carton) chilled, plain yogurt
1 can (8¼ ounces) chilled, crushed pineapple
1 teaspoon finely chopped candied ginger

Put yogurt, liquid and fruit of canned pineapple and ginger in blender. Whizz it. Strain (to remove unliquified pineapple fibers and ginger pieces). Serve at once or chill for later use. Makes two 8-ounce servings.

HAWAII'S ROYAL TEA

Anyone who has been a guest at Oahu Country Club and sipped pineapple mint iced tea on the club's lanai comes away impressed with the tea and this small Shangri-la.

2 quarts cold water   ⅓ cup sugar
⅓ cup loose, orange pekoe   Juice 3 lemons
    tea or 15 teabags   ⅓ cup pineapple juice
Fresh mint sprigs   Pineapple spears

In a saucepan bring 1 quart cold water to full rolling boil. Remove from heat; pour over tea. Stir and let stand 5 minutes. Stir and strain into pitcher containing 4 mint sprigs, sugar and 1 quart cold water. Stir to dissolve sugar. Cool it. Remove mint before chilling several hours or overnight. Stir in juices. Pour tea over ice cubes in tall glasses. Garnish each with a pineapple spear and mint sprig. Makes 6 to 8 servings.

COLA ADE

For teens and other teetotalers in the group.

1¼ cups (about 6 lemons)
   fresh lemon juice
1½ cups sugar
5 cups water

4 bottles or cans (about 12
   ounces each) cola
   carbonated beverage

Combine juice, sugar and water. Let stand overnight. Next day chill in refrigerator. Add cola beverage before serving. Pour over ice cubes in tall glasses. Makes about 12 servings.

SOUTHERN MINT CHILLER

The Southern hostess who made this for us says ice must be finely crushed and powdery—not in cubes or chunks. Pound it in heavy canvas bag if you haven't a crusher.

3 cups water
2 cups sugar
2 large handfuls tightly
   packed fresh mint
Juice 6 lemons (at least 1¼
   cups)

Grated peel and juice 2
   oranges (at least 1 cup)
Finely crushed ice
Soda water or ginger ale

Boil water and sugar together 5 minutes; pour over crushed cut mint leaves and stems. Cover tightly and steep until completely cooled, 1 hour or longer. Add peel and juice. Fill tall glasses with finely crushed ice; add 6 tablespoons mint syrup to each and fill with soda water or ginger ale. Serve with straws. Makes about 16 servings.

POOLSIDE FROSTY

Makes a good starter for a brunch also.

Place in blender container (in two portions) I can undiluted, frozen Daiquiri mix; 2 bananas, peeled and diced; 1 papaya, peeled, seeded and diced; 1 cup fresh pineapple pieces; ¼ cup sugar. Whizz until smooth. In two portions add 2 cups ice cubes and water to fill cups. Whizz until frothy. Serve in tall glasses over cracked ice. Garnish with lime slices. Makes 6 to 8 servings.

SPICED CRANBERRY TEA

⅓ cup tea leaves (black or a
 blend)
½ teaspoon cinnamon
¼ teaspoon nutmeg
1 teaspoon whole cloves
½ teaspoon allspice
3 cups freshly boiling water

½ to ¾ cup sugar
2 cups orange juice
1 quart cranberry juice
 cocktail
¼ cup lemon juice, or to
 taste

Tie tea and spices in small square of cloth. Place in teapot and pour in boiling water. Cover and steep 5 minutes. Remove teabag and add sugar. Stir until dissolved. Add remaining ingredients and chill. Pour over large chunk of ice or several trays of Double Flavor Ice Cubes* made of cold tea or cranberry juice cocktail. Makes about 3½ dozen punch cup servings.

CAN OPENER PUNCH

2 cans (6 ounces each) frozen
 lemonade concentrate
2 cans (6 ounces each) frozen
 orange juice concentrate
1 can (6 ounces) frozen
 limeade concentrate
2 cans (30 ounces each)
 pineapple juice

Angostura bitters†
4 bottles (about 1 quart each)
 ginger ale
1 bottle (about 1 quart)
 bitter-lemon carbonated
 beverage
Long spirals lemon peel or
 halved lemon slices

Mix fruit juices and pour over block of ice in punch bowl. Add generous dash of bitters and pour in ginger ale and bitter-lemon. Decorate with lemon peel or slices. Makes about 60 punch cup servings.

SANGRIA

Even non-wine fans enjoy this refreshing light wine punch from Spain. Perfect for summer meals. Use an ordinary dry red wine— a claret type or one of the Spanish or Italian reds—and keep the punch light on sugar.

2 *oranges*	4 *to 6 tablespoons sugar*
1 *bottle (⅘ quart) dry red*	2 *cups ice cubes*
wine	2 *tablespoons brandy, optional*
¼ *cup lemon juice*	1 *lemon, thinly sliced*

Cut peel from one orange in long spiral; drop into 1½-quart pitcher. Pour in wine. Squeeze juice from the peeled orange and half the other orange; add to wine. Blend in lemon juice, sugar, then ice cubes and brandy. Add lemon slices and remaining orange half, cut in thin slices. Chill 4 hours or more. Makes 1½ quarts.

PHILIP BROWN'S PUNCH

Hundreds of gallons of this wonderful dry punch have been consumed at the Browns' book parties over the years. A matchless combination!

4 *bottles dry white wine*	1 *cup lemon juice*
(Chablis, Folle Blanche and	1 *to 4 tablespoons sugar*
Pinot Chardonnay are all	2 *quarts charged water*
good choices)	*Ice*
1 *bottle (⅘ quart) brandy*	
1 *bottle (⅘ quart) Martinique*	
rum	

Mix together and pour over a large block of ice in punch bowl. This makes 60 punch cupfuls or enough to serve 30 persons with 2 cups each.

Note: Philip says this is a pretty heady mixture and you may easily double or even use four times as much wine as specified with the same amount of brandy and rum without affecting the flavor too much.

CHAMPAGNE WEDDING PUNCH

Next best to champagne itself for a wedding reception, or similar elegant occasions, is a good dry champagne punch with dry white wine used as a stretcher. Combine proportions that best suit your purse—but these are nice and the mixture is bubbly and light.

Decorated Ice Ring*
2 bottles (⅘ quart each) dry white wine (Pinot Chardonnay, Chablis, etc.)
1 cup brandy
3 bottles (⅘ quart each) very dry champagne

½ cup fresh lemon juice
⅓ cup sugar, or to taste
Whole, unhulled strawberries, long spirals lemon peel

If used, make decorated ice ring day before the party. Chill wine, brandy and champagne (see section on champagne in Philip S. Brown's Wines for the Cold Feast*). Mix lemon juice, sugar, brandy and wine; pour into punch bowl over large block of ice. Add strawberries and lemon peel and pour in champagne. Serve at once. (Decorated ice ring may replace ice and garnishes.) Makes 1 gallon or about 32 punch cup servings.

Note: Chill extra champagne and wine to add to punch as it is served if crowd is large.

DECORATED ICE RING

Day before party, put about 1-inch water in large metal ring mold; freeze. Top ice with a wreath of unhulled strawberries, thin half-slices lime and pin-size slivers lemon peel. Barely cover with water and freeze solid. Dip quickly in hot water to unmold. Float in punch bowl.

BRIDAL WREATH ICE RING

We have seen the suggestion of freezing orange blossoms, lily of the valley, stephanotis or other bridal flowers in an ice ring as a decoration for the wedding reception punch. We're not sure what it would do to the flavor—but it would be beautiful. You might freeze the flowers in a large ring of ice, set it on a tray lined with leaves and set punch bowl in that.

DOUBLE FLAVOR ICE CUBES

These chill drinks beautifully without diluting the flavors. Pour double-strength cold coffee or tea, limeade, lemonade, cranberry cocktail, orange juice or orange drink, grape juice, etc., into ice cube trays with dividers in place. Freeze solid.

DECORATED ICE CUBES

Place in each section of ice cube trays the following, or other garnishes, choosing the color and flavor that will complement your particular drink: unhulled strawberries, blackberries, boysenberries, blueberries, raspberries, cherries, grapes; slices of orange, lemon, lime or cucumber; chunks of pineapple, watermelon, honeydew, cantaloupe, peaches, nectarines; mint or fragrant geranium leaves; rose petals; small daisies; tarragon or parsley sprigs, ad infinitum. Fill with water and freeze solid.

CHAPTER X

Wines for the Cold Feast ⌒

BY PHILIP S. BROWN

The choice of wines to serve with cold foods is, like all wine selection, a matter of personal preference. There are no hard and fast rules; if you like it, it's right. In general, however, most people prefer lighter wines with such fare, and many feel that the cold buffet is the one place where rosé wine is the perfect beverage. The following suggestions are just that. No brand names are specified, as there are many excellent makers of each type of wine mentioned. By sampling and comparing you will find the one you prefer.

Champagne has many advocates, and they have a very good point, as there is something about that wine which seems to enhance chilled foods, from hors d'oeuvres to dessert. When serving champagne to begin with or throughout the meal, choose a Brut or Extra Dry, as they go well with everything. If it is to be served only with a sweet dessert, choose one of the sweeter types. In any case, keep it cold and keep it coming, for even the most temperate of your guests will consume surprising quantities of it. One bottle will fill about six glasses, so figure accordingly. Although it is not necessary to serve the best and most expensive brands of champagne, do not serve the cheapest either. Rather, select one in the middle range, either from France or California, and be sure that it is bottle-fermented, not made by the bulk fermentation method. Chill a few bottles at a time in a bucket or tub filled with ice and water; the idea is to chill it quickly and well. Serve it in tulip-shaped champagne glasses rather than the saucer-shaped ones, which allow the bubbles to dissipate too quickly.

If champagne is not to your taste or pocketbook, there are many other white wines, sans bubbles, which go well with many chilled foods. Chablis, the very dry white Burgundy, is ideal with all fish and most light poultry, and is a fine apéritif wine as well. Chablis from California is extremely variable. The best of it, although not as dry and austere as the French Chablis, is also excellent with cold foods. From the Loire Valley of France come such lovely white wines as Pouilly Fumé, Muscadet, Sancerre, and Quincy, all of which are superb, though Quincy may be hard to find. Vouvray, also from the Loire region, is another good choice, but be sure to buy a "Nature," as other types may be too sweet. All of these wines should be served chilled in regular large "all-purpose" wineglasses.

The fruity wines of Alsace, the Moselle and the Rhine are also appealing, although some Moselles and many Rhines may be too sweet. Gewurztraminer, whether from California or France, is always popular with cold foods, and especially so in summer. Riesling or (in California) Johannisberg Riesling is also refreshing and well liked by nearly everyone. The Riesling grape is, of course, the variety from which all Moselle wines and most of the better Rhine wines are made. Another favorite is Sylvaner, which also comes from either France or California, and is drier and lighter than the Rieslings. Similar white wines from California are Green Hungarian and Emerald Riesling, both of which are light and pleasant. All of these wines should be chilled before serving, and should be presented in Rhine wineglasses with long stems, if you have them. If not, use your "all-purpose" glasses.

As I mentioned above, a great many wine-lovers feel that a chilled rosé is ideal with cold meals. Besides being light, with a pleasant and flowery bouquet, rosé wines are lovely to look at; their delicate pink color is most attractive on a warm summer evening. They go especially well with such things as ham, corned beef and more highly seasoned dishes. One of the Portuguese rosés is the largest-selling imported wine in America, believe it or not. The most famous of French rosé wines is Tavel, but there are a number of others which are worthy of consideration—Anjou, Sancerre and Provence for example. Speaking very generally, California rosés are less sweet than those from Europe, and the best of them are made from the Grenache and Gamay grapes. They should be very well chilled and served in "all-purpose" wineglasses.

With cold entrées which are relatively heavy, like roast beef, duck, liver pâtés and such things, I prefer a light red wine, and of those

Beaujolais is by far the best known and most popular. Wine simply labeled "Beaujolais" varies widely in quality, and should always be drunk very young—not over two years old and preferably younger. The wines from the Beaujolais region which are entitled to other appellations (Brouilly, Chenas, Chiroubles, Côte de Brouilly, Fleurie, Julienas, Morgon, Moulin-à-Vent and Saint-Amour) are far more reliable and will live considerably longer in the bottle. True Beaujolais wines are made from the Gamay grape, but in California they may be, and are, made from whatever grapes the vintner chooses to use. Consequently there is a great range of flavor, color and aroma among them. The best ones are labeled Gamay Beaujolais or simply Gamay, which indicates that they contain at least 51 per cent of wine made from the Gamay grape. All Beaujolais are best when served very slightly chilled or at cellar temperature—60 to 65 degrees F.—and they should be poured into "all-purpose" wineglasses.

Other light red wines from Burgundy, such as Mercurey, Santenay, Savigny and Volnay, are splendid companions for the heavier cold entrées. They should not be chilled. From Italy come many wines which are suitable for this type of food, notably Soave (white) and Valpolicella (red), which are readily available in most parts of this country. Switzerland also produces some eminently satisfactory wines, mainly white, the best known of which are Neuchatel and Dezaley, but really good ones are hard to find as most of them are consumed by the Swiss. Most Spanish table wines are too heavy for this sort of food, but a pitcher of Sangria, the great Spanish summer beverage, would make a good accompaniment, especially if the meal is to be served alfresco.

To sum it up, in my opinion cold food calls for light wines, whether white, red or rosé.

CHAPTER XI

12 Party Menus ～

WINTER HOLIDAY BUFFET

Holiday Drinks or Punch
Roquefort Mushrooms*   Hot Empanaditas[1]   Gravlax*
Pepper Roast*   Ham with Chaud Froid Glaze*
Hot and Mild Mustards   Pickles and Celery   Ginger Mint Relish*
French Potato Salad*   Avocado Mousse Picante*
Assorted Breads   Crisp Rolls
Fruit Cake   Ruth Bateman's Cafe Jamaica*
Coffee

SUMMER BUFFET

Chilled White Wine
Pick-up Melon-and-Prosciutto Sticks   Crudités with Tapenade*
Chicken Salad Amandine*   Salmon in Aspic*
Vegetable Bouquet Platter
(Ring of assorted Vegetables à la Grecque*
centered with Masked Cauliflower*)
Bread Sticks   Sweet Butter   Crisp Hot Biscuits
Tortoni Ribbon Cake*   Coffee

[1] Tiny half-moon pastries filled with spicy shrimp or meat filling.

LUNCHEON FOR THE LADIES

Hot Sherry Consommé
Breast of Chicken Jeannette*   Croissants
Hot Green Beans Polonaise[2]
Orange Salad Rosemary*
Melon Ice*   Coffee or Tea

TEA FOR FIFTY

Pink Ribbons*   Egg Rings*   Ham in Brioche*
Salted Nuts   Brandied Dates[3]
Mocha Puffs[4]   Miniature Fruit Tarts
Hot Tea or Spiced Cranberry Tea*   Coffee

SIT-DOWN DINNER

Champagne
Veal and Ham Pâté, Mosaic*   Sliced French Rolls and Butter
Dilled Shrimp Avocado*
Roast Rack of Lamb   Parsley Potato and Carrot Balls
Spinach and Mushroom Salad*
Celestial Strawberries* or Mousse au Chocolat*
Demitasse

[2] Whole green beans topped with bread crumbs sauteed in butter until golden, parsley added.
[3] Pit fresh dates and soak overnight in brandy.
[4] Tiny Cream Puff Shells* filled with whipped cream sweetened and flavored with a packet of pre-melted chocolate and powdered coffee.

TERRACE SUPPER

A Pitcher of Chilled Rosé or Sangria*
Swordfish Escabeche*   Melba Toast   Soused Camembert*
Stuffed Rock Cornish Hens*
Saffron Rice Salad[5]   Tomatoes Monterey*
Viennese Meringue Torte*
Coffee

SCANDINAVIAN SMORGASBORD

Skal
Cheers!
with
Iced Akvavit   Chilled Beer   Dry Martinis, on-the-Rocks
and
Selections of Herring
Pickled Salt Herring   Herring with Sour Cream
(Inglad Sill)   (Sill med Sur Gradde)

Herring Salad, Stockholm*
(Sillsalad)

[5] Rice cooked with saffron powder to color, then tossed with Sauce Vinaigrette,*
puffed raisins and pine nuts.

The Chilled Buffet

Iced Swedish Caviar
(Kaviar)
Anchovied Eggs*
(Fyllda Ägg)
Westcoast Salad[6]
(Väskustsallad)
Liver Paste*
(Leverpastej)
Vinegar Beets*
(Inlagd Rödbeta)
Pressed Lamb Roll*
(Får Rulle)

Sliced Smoked Salmon
(Lax)
Jansson's Temptation[7]
(Jansson's Frestelse)
Cucumber Salad*
(Agurkesalat)
Cold Beef Tongue*
(Oxtunga)
Danish Macaroni Salad*
(Makaronisalat)
Jellied Pork and Veal*
(Sylta)

Mustardy Crumb Crusted Baked Ham
(Skinka)
Cherry Tomatoes   Olives   Sweet Gherkins   Radishes   Celery
Danish Pumpernickel   Butter Balls   Swedish Rye Bread

The Hot Buffet

Danish Meatballs
(Frikadeller)
Danish Carmelized Potatoes
(Brunede Kartofler)
Sweet-sour Red Cabbage
(Rødkal)

[6] Westcoast Salad, a famed Swedish dish made with cold boiled seafood, raw
mushrooms, tomatoes, lettuce and dill flavoring in the dressing.
[7] Jansson's Temptation is a popular smörgåsbord dish, a delicious casserole
made of anchovies, potatoes and onions baked in cream.

Dessert

Sour Cream Pound Cake
(Kermakaaku)
Lemon Chiffon Pudding, Red Raspberry Sauce*
(Citron Fromage*)
Assorted Cheeses
Smörgåsbord Coffee[8]   Cherry Heering Liqueur

Note: Take as much or as little as you wish, but do change plates for each grouping . . . the types of food and different serving temperatures demand a clean sweep.

Although consisting of many items, a smörgåsbord buffet has the advantage of early preparation for most foods; others are often available at a delicatessen.

A RUSSIAN BUFFET

The Zakuska Table

A Carafe of Ice-cold Vodka   A Carafe of Chilled Dry Martinis
Herring with Mustard Sauce
Fresh Beluga Caviar[9]
Smoked Salmon, Vinaigrette
Swiss Cheese   Dill Pickles
Salad Olivier*   Cucumbers in Sour Cream
Pickled Artichoke Hearts   Pickled Mushrooms*
Hot Miniature Meatballs, Tomato Sauce
Russian Pumpernickel   Butter Curls   French Bread

[8] Swedish coffee is served strong and hot, and is very important on a smörgåsbord menu.

[9] Pressed black caviar and red caviar are less expensive and more readily available.

The Dining Room Buffet

Rare Fillet of Beef Stroganoff
Green Barley Casserole
Limestone Lettuce with Egg Dressing*
Orange Trifle*   Strawberries Romanoff, Cuyamaca*
Strong Tea, Lemon Slices   Cordials

AFTER-THE-THEATER
Supper for Four

Chinese Chicken Salad*
(Sow See Gai)
Lichee Pink Snow, Almond Custard Sauce*
Fortune Cookies   Almond Cookies
Chinese Tea

KAMAAINA[10] DINNER
ON A HAWAIIAN LANAI

Cocktails of your Choice
with Pupus
(Appetizers)
Pineapple Pupus* Sashimi* Macadamia Nuts
Nasturtium Salad*
Teriyaki Steak
Steamed Rice   Broiled Tomatoes
Hearts and Guavas*
Hawaii's Royal-Tea*   Kona Coffee

10 *Kamaaina:* a long-time resident of Hawaii.

AN INFORMAL LUNCHEON

Iced Avgolemono*
Euphrates Wafers   Sesame Crisps   Melba Toast
Greek Salata*
Hot Garlic Toast
Angel Pie, Country Squire*
Tea   Coffee   Pastel Mints

DINNER FOR SIX

Sweet or Dry Vermouth, on-the-Rocks, Lemon Twist
with
Trout Antipasto*
French Bread   Butter
Verdicchio de Jesi[11]   Risotto Milanese[12]
Vitello Tonnato*
Artichoke Hearts, Lemon Butter
Assorted Cheeses
Angela Pia*
Fruits in Season
Strega[13]   Coffee   Galliano[13]

[11] Verdicchio de Jesi is a light, very dry wine with a spicy quality. It is produced
near Ancona in Italy.
[12] A saffron-flavored rice dressed with Parmesan cheese.
[13] Strega and Galliano are Italian liqueurs with an anise flavor.

Glossary and Shopper's Guide ⟨⟩

Angostura bitters: An aromatic preparation of water, alcohol, gentian, harmless vegetable-flavoring extracts and coloring. It makes an excellent seasoning and flavoring agent.

Bean threads, Saifun: Nylon-like noodles made from ground mung peas, quite white, transparent and very hard. Unless deep-fried, they must be soaked before using. They offer a cellophane airiness to oriental foods.

Brown mustard: Usually the German-type, rather strong in flavor, darkish in color. Best with sharply seasoned foods like sausages and sauerkraut.

Capers: Flower buds of the wild caper bush, which grows in southern France, Algeria and Asia Minor countries. Pickled in vinegar and used as a relish and in sauces.

Small yellow hot (chili) pepper: Known also by Incan name, Aji, and Spanish name, Amarillo chili, which means yellow pepper. It is fiery and unlike large, sweet, cool variety. Sold fresh in some metropolitan areas or canned, packed in jars.

Chinese 5-Spice: A ready-mixed powder of ground spices, composed of star anise, anise pepper, fennel, cloves and cinnamon. It is fragrant, pungent and to be used sparingly. If unavailable, substitute with cinnamon, or equal parts cinnamon, allspice and ground anise.

Chinese (hot) chili sauce: A very hot sauce made with small red chili peppers, fruit and garlic flavors. Used sparingly in oriental cooking. If unavailable, Mexican hot sauce (Salsa Jalapeña) or Louisiana hot sauce may be substituted.

Cilantro, coriander, Chinese parsley: A fresh herb with broad, flat serrated leaves, quite different from American double-curled parsley in appearance and pungent flavor. To be used sparingly in oriental and Latin American cooking.

Daikon, Japanese white radish: Has flavor similar to small white turnips and icicle white radishes, but hotter. Used in soups, shredded or thinly sliced, as a relish or salad component.

Dijon mustard: A prepared mustard made with white wine, named for Dijon, France, where it originated. Domestic Dijon type is less potent than the imported.

Creole horseradish: A prepared horseradish, containing horseradish and distilled vinegar, salt and preservative; no artificial flavoring added. Used in creole cookery; produced by Zatarains in Louisiana.

Creole mustard: A prepared, very hot mustard made from a unique variety of ground mustard seeds, distilled vinegar, salt and preservative. Used in creole cookery; produced by Zatarains in Louisiana.

English mustard: A sharp, vinegary mustard with a distinctive sweetness.

Ginger root: A knobbly tuber. When peeled, sliced, shredded or crushed it releases a fresh, pungent aroma and taste to meats, vegetables, seafoods, soups and desserts; the ground ginger does not produce the same quality. Its spicy flavor neutralizes fish odors, and in oriental cooking is always used with fish dishes. If a slice is required in a recipe, it should be of an inch in diameter and up to ⅛ inch thick. Ginger juice is most readily obtained by cutting a piece of root and squeezing it in garlic press. Ginger root may be stored about 3 weeks in refrigerator, or placed in a plastic bag in freezer (shred it while still frozen). Most often used in oriental cooking. If unavailable, rinsed, preserved ginger may be substituted.

Galax leaves: An evergreen herb whose shiny, shapely leaves are widely used in decorations. Other leaves . . . ivy, geranium, lemon, etc., may be used.

Greek feta cheese: A white, crumbly cheese made from goat's or sheep's milk. Greek Gruyère, Graviéra, is often used instead.

Hoisin sauce: A thick, spicy sauce, somewhat like catsup; made with oriental spices, soy beans, garlic and chili. It is sweet and spicy, called by a variety of names and used in oriental cooking and as a table condiment for oriental food.

Hungarian paprika: Hungarian name for sweet red (rose) pepper used traditionally in *paprikash* and other Hungarian dishes. It's sweeter and hotter than the mild Spanish paprika.

Kosher salt, sea salt: Both are coarse salts esteemed by epicures. Kosher salt available in kosher food stores, fancy food stores and many supermarkets. Sea salt is coarser, perhaps a little saltier and generally found only in fancy food shops.

Lichee, lychee, litchi: An exotic oriental fruit available fresh in fine food shops in July. Delicately flavored, similar to the grape. Expensive. More generally available in cans imported from the Orient and Philippines. The amount of liquid and sweetness of canned fruit varies from cannery to cannery. Used in salads, or with chicken, duck or pork, or as a sweet.

Louisiana hot sauce: A very hot liquid pepper sauce made of fermented green and sometimes red peppers. Often used in southern and creole cooking.

Maggi seasoning: A liquid seasoning or flavoring sauce made of vegetable proteins, water and salt. Enhances the flavor of foods rather than adding any flavor of its own.

Saifun: See Bean threads

Sake: Known as a Japanese rice wine, sake is technically a beer. It does lack carbon dioxide as in creamy beers, and it is stronger than most beers, having 14 to 16 per cent alcohol by volume. By the first taste it is sweet, and as an aftertaste bitter. Sake is used as a beverage or in oriental cooking; dry sherry may be used instead.

Salsa Jalapeña and Mexican hot sauce: Salsa Jalapeña is a green or red relish made with jalapeñas, very hot peppers. Mexican hot sauce, sometimes called taco sauce, is hot also and made with puréed fiery peppers. Used in Latin American cooking.

Seasoned salt: Salt with a special blend of spices and seasonings added. Packed by Lawry's Foods. *Seasoning salts,* or salt with special seasonings added, and they vary with the packer, are packed by French's, Schilling (McCormick & Co.), among others.

Sesame oil: A heavy, strong oil made from toasted white sesame seeds. Used for its nutlike flavor and fragrance in soups, cold dishes and with chicken. Use it sparingly in oriental cooking.

Sesame seeds: Little flat seeds, either black or white, used in baked goods and many oriental dishes. When toasted they have a rich, nutlike flavor.

Shrimp chips: A product similar to potato chips; made from a combination of tapioca flour, shrimp and spices, sliced and deep-fried. Used with Indonesian foods.

Soy sauce: The sauce referred to in the recipes in this book is salty and dark, and marketed generally for cooking and as a table condiment. Made of soybeans, wheat, yeast and salt plus caramel for color.

Spice Parisienne: A special blend of nutmeg, cloves, white and black pepper and herbs packed by Spice Islands. Excellent for canapé spreads and pâtés, savory sauces, meatballs and loaves, etc.

Star anise cloves: Each clove is a dime-size eight-pointed star of licorice-flavor . . . quite strong. Use sparingly in oriental cooking.

Truffles: Distinctive, pungent fungi that grow underground especially in southern France and Italy. Highly esteemed for their aromatic flavor in sauces, pâtés, omelets and in classic decorations for aspics. Expensive. Either fresh or canned available in fancy food shops.

SHOPPER'S *Guide*
(*General Foreign Foods*)

Many of the foreign or unusual ingredients are available generally in supermarkets throughout the country. Others will be found in specialty shops and fine food stores. The following list is representative but not at all inclusive.

Boston, Massachusetts

S. S. Pierce Company
133 Brookline Avenue
02215

Chicago, Illinois

The Pantry
Marshall Field and Co.
111 N. State Street
60602

Stop and Shop
16 W. Washington Blvd.
60602

Dallas, Texas

The Epicure Shop
Neiman-Marcus
Main at Ervay
75201

Denver, Colorado

May D & F Gourmet Shop
16th and Tremont Place
80202

Houston, Texas

European Import Store
910 Preston Street
P. O. Box 2205
77001

Los Angeles, California

Jurgensen's Grocery Company
409 N. Beverly Drive
Beverly Hills
90210

New Orleans, Louisiana

D. H. Holmes
819 Canal Street
70112

New York, New York

Bloomingdale Brothers
Lexington Avenue, 59th Street
10017

Hammacher Schlemmer & Co.,
Inc.
145 E. 57th Street
10022

Vendome Table Delicacies
415 Madison Avenue
10017

Abraham & Straus
402 Fulton Street
Brooklyn, N.Y.
11201

San Francisco, California

Simon Brothers
2829 California Street
94115

The City of Paris
Geary and Stockton Street
94108

Seattle, Washington

Frederick & Nelson
Fifth and Pine
98101

Specialties. Mail order catalogue by request

(Chinese)

Lee's Agency
715 Sacramento Street
San Francisco, California
94108

(Indonesian)

Holland-American Market and Importing Co., Inc.
10333–10343 E. Artesia Blvd.
Bellflower, California
90706

(Oriental)

Cathay Food Products, Inc.
115 Broadway
New York, New York
10006

Index